The Untold Truth About Salvation

The Untold Truth About Salvation

What you don't hear in Churches

By

RANDY CHESLER

XULON ELITE

Xulon Press Elite
2301 Lucien Way #415
Maitland, FL 32751
407.339.4217
www.xulonpress.com

© 2022 by Randy Chesler

All rights reserved solely by the author. The author guarantees all contents are original and do not infringe upon the legal rights of any other person or work. No part of this book may be reproduced in any form without the permission of the author. The views expressed in this book are not necessarily those of the publisher.

Due to the changing nature of the Internet, if there are any web addresses, links, or URLs included in this manuscript, these may have been altered and may no longer be accessible. The views and opinions shared in this book belong solely to the author and do not necessarily reflect those of the publisher. The publisher, therefore, disclaims responsibility for the views or opinions expressed within the work.

Unless otherwise indicated, Scripture quotations taken from the English Standard Version (ESV). Copyright © 2001 by Crossway, a publishing ministry of Good News Publishers. Used by permission. All rights reserved.

Paperback ISBN-13: 978-1-66286-084-3
Ebook ISBN-13: 978-1-66286-085-0

Table of Contents

WHY THIS BOOK	ix
INTRODUCTION	xiii
UNLOCKING THE MYSTERY OF MAN	1
FREE CHOICE	15
THE UNTOLD TRUTH ABOUT SALVATION	37
TO BELIEVE OR NOT TO BELIEVE	73
WHO WILL INHERIT THE KINGDOM OF GOD?	85
WHAT REALLY HAPPENS WHEN WE DIE?	101
WHAT IS AN IMMORTAL SOUL?	107
WHAT ABOUT HELL?	113
REPENTANCE	145
BAPTISM, HOLY SPIRIT, AND FIRE	157
JUDGMENT	185
REVELATION	199
SUMMARY	259

WHY THIS BOOK?

For most of us who have read the Bible or been to a Christian Church, we generally share the same beliefs and philosophies about Jesus and Salvation. Although, there still seems to be a lot of confusion and unanswered questions as it relates to these beliefs. And the more I thought about it, the more I realized that some of these ideas and philosophies just aren't adding up. I kept getting that feeling that something just isn't right. Things aren't making any sense. Something seems to be missing!

Then, as time went by, it just kept nagging at me more and more. Some of the things we've heard for years just weren't adding up. They didn't make any sense. Until eventually I couldn't ignore it anymore. So, I did a deep dive into some of these common beliefs and ideas. Then, I found out that a lot of what we've been taught about God and the Bible just isn't true. The Bible is very clear, easy to understand, yet some of the things we've heard or been taught is in direct conflict to what the Bible actually says.

For instance, what happens when we die? I mean, what **really** happens when we die...and what happens to all of our family and friends when they die?

It's not beyond our grasp to get a sense of what the Bible is trying to say. There are a lot of great tools that can help navigate the Bible in an orderly manner and search out the answers you need.

So, what does happen when we die? Well, the common Christian belief is that our soul goes to another place. And we hope it's the right place and not the bad one.

This is just one of the many questions that was nagging at me. I wanted answers, I wanted to know. So, I went straight to the Bible to see what the Bible actually says. Then, using one of those tools I referenced earlier, I was able to search the entire Bible in just minutes to find all the scriptures that used the word "soul" or "immortal soul". When I was done, I was shocked at what I discovered. You will be surprised to know that **NO WHERE** in the Bible does it even mention an immortal soul. Then I continued to look up the word soul. I found that a lot of translations only use the word creature. But in other translations where you find the word soul, the original Hebrew word is creature. You can research that on your own by using a Biblical study tool called a Concordance, in which you can find the original meaning of any word in the Bible. Or you can research it online. That's how I found out that the word soul only means creature. The same word was used for creatures of the sea, animal creatures, bird creatures, & human creatures, but **NEVER** immortal creatures.

These conflicting ideas between what we've been taught and what the Bible actually says goes way beyond what happens when we die. What about salvation? What is God's real plan for Salvation? And what does accepting Jesus have anything to do with all that? What about Hell? Who goes there? It's not who you think. Where does free choice come into play and what about the Kingdom of God?

These common beliefs about God, salvation, along with other concepts, as it relates to the Christian experience, are just not adding up. But now that I know it is not that difficult to look into these things on my own, I can finally get to the bottom of all these nagging feelings and unanswered questions as I find out what the Bible actually says.

INTRODUCTION

What I am about to tell you may shock you, it may surprise you, it might make you angry, and your first reaction might be to stand in dis-belief and deny it. But a lot of what we've been taught about God and the Bible is simply **NOT** true. It is nothing more than urban myth. I'm about to show you what the Bible actually says and what it doesn't say. These are **NOT** Randy's ideas or interpretation. It is all there, right in front of your eyes, in black and white, but a lot of people just read right over it and ignore the simple truth.

Have you ever just read the Bible to **prove to yourself** what it actually says? Have you ever read through it without adding a "yeah, but" or "I think it means…" after every clear statement? I am not talking about reading it through like a novel or following along in church. I mean taking the time to actually read it for what it says and putting a period after every clear statement. The Bible is very clear, easy to understand, but what adds confusion are the "yeah buts…" and the "I think it means…".

If something doesn't seem clear, then research what it means and compare it to other clear statements. If what you think the Bible means contradicts scriptures that are very clear, then it cannot mean what you think it means. In this case, the clear statements are always right, because the Bible does not contradict itself.

At this point, you may want to start taking notes and write down your questions as you're reading this, because you will definitely have questions. And you may want to write down any objections; because you will have plenty of those as well, especially when you start to see some discrepancies between what you've heard or been taught and what the Bible actually says.

Let's start by talking about what we've been taught. Someone in your life told you about God or taught you about the Bible. That someone could have been a parent, a teacher, a mentor, a friend, or perhaps a pastor. Of course, you believed them because you loved them and trusted them. How could they be wrong, you looked up to them, after all they were the expert on the subject. All normal questions that run through your mind. However, they were **WRONG!** They taught you what they've been taught and so-on. But what does God and the Bible actually say?

In order to discover and understand what the Bible actually says, we have to overcome some obstacles, some challenges, and some mental blocks. **The first obstacle** to overcome is ourselves. Sometimes **WE** get in the way. We get stuck in our own beliefs and our own thoughts. Sometimes we have pre-conceived ideas about God or the Bible. And we let certain concepts, words, or expressions get in the way. The first thing we need to do is admit that there is a possibility that what we've been taught could be wrong. No one lied to you, no one tricked you and it certainly wasn't malicious. They just taught you what they've been taught. Besides, I just said admit the **possibility**, because there is always that possibility that what we've been taught could be wrong. If you have a thought or an idea that pops into your head, ask yourself, "where did that idea come from?" Is it actually in the Bible or did someone just tell you it was in the Bible? For instance, the idea of an immortal soul can't be found anywhere in the Bible.

The second obstacle to understanding the Bible is that it uses a lot of symbolism, imagery, metaphors, and poetry. So, when you're reading the Bible, it helps to understand that it is not always literal. Sometimes it uses metaphors or imagery to paint a mental picture to get the point across. Keep that in mind as it applies to the context.

The third obstacle to understanding the Bible is that it was written in a different time and different culture than what we are dealing with today. So, when you're reading the Bible, keep that in mind as it relates to the subject matter, the audience, and the culture at the time.

Another obstacle to understanding the Bible is that it was translated into English. This is probably the BIGGEST obstacle of them all, since the Bible was not originally written in English. The Old Testament was written in Hebrew and the New Testament in Greek.

Sometime back in 1604, King James of England had this "bright idea" that if he translated the Bible into English, it would prove his supremacy. So, he used 47 scholars and theologians to accomplish this task over the next 7 years. Then, in 1611 it was complete, and the first King James Bible was published. Although William Tyndale translated the New Testament from Greek into English back in 1525, he was executed for heresy less than 10 years later. Nonetheless, king James and his team ended up using some, if not all, of Tyndale's works.

Why is the English translation such a big obstacle? Because the English version, more specifically Old English, uses old fashioned words, some of which are not even used in modern English today. For instance, words like repent, baptize, hell, sin, gospel and holy, just to name a few, are Old English words. All of these words sound soooo "religious". Are they really or are they just Old English words? These words are typically only used in Church. However, when you take Old English words from the past and try to use them in a Modern English environment today, the meanings of these words get skewed.

The real definitions of some of these Old English words are:

Repent   -   Change your mind.
Hell   -   Cover or Conceal.
Sin   -   Miss the mark.
Gospel   -   Good News.
Holy   -   Set Apart.
Baptize -   Immerse.

While researching all of this, it occurred to me one day that there is so much confusion about the Bible throughout the many different Christian beliefs and denominations. There are differences about who and what God is, His purpose for man, God's plan of salvation, who is going to heaven and who is going to Hell and so many other ideas involving God and the Bible. Whereas Paul said in **I Corinthians 14:33 (ESV)**, "God is not a God of confusion but of peace". So, why is there so much confusion? Well, if you think about it, Satan is the master of confusion, the king of chaos. So, if it's not God causing confusion, then it must be Satan who is deceiving churches from within, even those churches who claim to be the "one true" Church.

So, let's read the Bible and see what it actually says...

UNLOCKING
THE MYSTERY OF MAN

The key to unlocking the mystery of man is buried somewhere in the Garden of Eden. So, to understand God's plan and His overall purpose for man, we have to go all the way back to the Garden.

Now, if you've already tuned me out, rolled your eyes, or put up those walls and said, "that's just Randy talking, what does he know", then you've already closed your mind. If that's the case, you probably won't hear a word I'm saying. But, what if…and I mean what if what I am saying is **by revelation of God**, then you may want to stick around awhile because you could be missing out on something **BIG**.

It is easy to stay with our current belief system, even if we are wrong, because it is a safe place. However, being open to challenges to our beliefs is part of what strengthens us and contributes to meaningful change. If you are still with me and still listening and wanting to learn about what could change your entire life forever, we are about to take a journey back to the Garden of Eden.

The Bible communicates a sense of God, His personality, His character, and His nature. There are plenty of scriptures and stories you can read as well as situations in the Bible that describe God and define His personality and His character.

Then, after reading about God and getting to know Him and seeing what He's all about, do you think God is an impulsive God, hasty, spur-of-the-moment kind of God or is He well planned out, organized, and works by design? While you're thinking about that, let's go back to the beginning and take a look at **Genesis 1:1–31 (ESV)**. In verses: 2-4, "the spirit moved upon the face of the waters. And God said, let there be light: and there was light. And God saw the light, that it was good".

The creation, as we know it, started here on the first day when God said, "let there be light". As precise as the light had to be, as detailed as it was, do you think God just threw it together in the hopes it would work? Or did He have a plan so the sun would be the exact distance from the earth and just the right size to supply the perfect amount of heat and light, so the earth would not burn up or freeze over? And it could not be too dark or too bright either.

Do you think God came up with a design plan long before He uttered those words "let there be light"? Or did He wake up one day and say, "you know what bro,

I think I'm gonna make the light shine tomorrow and maybe by the end of the week I'll put together some kind of breathing, thinking doll and call it human"? Most engineers, designers and inventors come up with a plan first, then map things out or draw up a design before they even get started with the building phase. Based on multiple examples and situations in the Bible involving God, we can see that He definitely plans things out. He's **NOT** just making this stuff up as He goes along.

The first example that comes to mind is Noah's Ark. God designed the entire Ark in detail to make sure it was going to be the right fit. It had to be big enough to hold all the animals and strong enough to withstand the floods. Then He told Noah how to build it, including what materials to get from Home Depot, along with the exact dimensions. Sounds like it was well planned out.

Let's get to the part where we look at what the Bible actually says. For one, we have established that God is a planner. But, even if He just threw together creation on a whim, the one thing we do know for sure, from the Bible, is that at the end of the first day "God saw the light, that it was good". In other words, He was happy with the outcome and well pleased with His work. Light was good and now He can move on to phase two (day two). That is when God separated the water from the earth and in v10 God "saw that it was good". Now God is ready for phase three (day three). This is where God creates grass, herbs, fruits, and plants. And, once again, in v12 God "saw that it was good".

This pattern continues throughout the rest of creation. Then, fast forwarding to day six in v26-31. Just like God made all the plants after their kind, God also made the fish of the sea, the fowl of the air and the beasts of the earth all after their kind. But, when it came time to create man in v26, "God said, let us make man in our image, after our likeness". Basically, God was making man after the God kind. In effect, He was reproducing Himself through man. Then in v31, "God saw everything that He had made, and behold, it was **VERY GOOD**". Sounds like God was **very pleased** with His work. He did **exactly** what He planned to do. Now, it is time for God to sit back and enjoy his handy-work and take a day off.

When God made us, He made us human. He designed us and created us weak, easily over-powered by sin. Then He gave us human nature and He said it was **VERY GOOD**. That human nature includes all the emotions that go with being human, such as happy, sad, fear, disgust, anger, and surprise. These emotions are linked to hormones and chemical reactions in the brain, all designed by God as part of the human model. Once we have a chemical reaction that generates an emotion, then that emotion sparks a feeling. Feelings are the conscious experience of what we feel when we get one of these emotions. These feelings are shaped by our beliefs, life experiences, memories, and thoughts that are connected to that emotion.

For instance, if we get angry and then we start to **feel** hatred and our human reaction to that hatred is to kill someone, it was God who created us with the emotion of anger, and He said it was **VERY GOOD**. And the human reaction of killing would not exist unless God made it possible by creating man weaker than sin.

I am not saying killing is good, but when God designed us, He gave us emotions that would eventually explode into negative feelings and reactions. It was inevitable that humans would eventually mess up and make some really bad choices and **God knew that**. Yet, He said it was **VERY GOOD**. We turned out exactly how God intended...humans capable of bad choices. That is God's human design.

Oh Noooo! God wouldn't do that, would He? Well, He did! If He didn't do it, then who did? God made us, right? Then the **potential** for killing, the **potential** for evil deeds was built into the human design created by God. God expected it. If that wasn't His design or His plan, then what happened? Did God mess up somehow? Or did someone steal His plans and sabotage His work?

We see that God is well planned out and organized, so what did happen?

1. Did God **plan** on Adam messing up?
2. Or Did Adam mess up God's **plan**?

The common belief is that Adam messed up God's plan. If that's the case, then God's plan must have been really weak. God couldn't even get past the first humans before His plan got trashed and He had to start over with a backup plan. Then again, according to common belief, it doesn't look like His backup plan is working out so well either. But, if Adam did mess up God's plan, it was still God who came up with a plan so weak that Adam could mess it up or He created Adam so weak that he couldn't stick to a plan. Either way, it was still God who put all this in motion. So, it must have been intentional. He planned on Adam messing up. Otherwise, if He didn't do it intentionally, what happened? Did something go wrong? Did God make a mistake?

After God took all that time to plan and organize His creation, as thorough as He was at designing every detail, it doesn't make any sense that God would turn His entire creation, His plan over to Adam and risk everything, just to have Adam mess it up before it even got started. Unless God knew what would happen and He planned it that way.

Although, some may argue it's about choice and we "choose" to make bad choices. And they argue that Adam made a really bad choice and messed up God's plan. Did Adam single handedly ruin God's plan? That does not even make any sense. It was God's plan "for God's sake!" So, whatever happened, including Adam messing up, must have all been part of God's plan.

God is **NOT** going to allow our choices to change the direction of His original plan. All roads still lead back to God. It was God who made us weak in the first place, easily over-powered by sin, and capable of bad choices. And it was God who gave us the option to make those bad choices by giving us free choice. And the choices we make are based on emotions and feelings God gave us, as well as any life experiences and knowledge we've acquired in this environment that God put us in, without giving us a choice. In other words, these were all God's decisions, God's choices, God's plan in the first place.

Besides, is God's plan about our free choice or is God's plan about **GOD** and His free choice. That choice, that decision He made when He came up with a plan a long time ago, before He even created man with free choice.

God certainly could have designed us without emotions, so it would be impossible to make bad choices, but he didn't. Being human means that **WE WILL** make a bad choice eventually. It was all part of God's original plan that He built into the human design, which He said was **VERY GOOD**. God knew what He was doing, He knew we would mess up, in fact He expected it. And yet, He still said it was **VERY GOOD**.

Before we talk about free choice in the next section, we briefly mentioned it above as part of how God designed us. The Bible never talks about it, but it's obvious we have independent thought. And God does not control our actions. Free choice is the option (permission) to make good or bad choices on our own. Otherwise, it would not be a choice.

While we are traveling down this road of life, we can kill, steal, worship Satan all we want, and God is not going to stop us. For instance, Cain killing his brother Abel. God did not stop him. Cain had a bad attitude, and he was jealous of his brother. Then Cain had an emotional reaction and lost his temper. Had God not made human nature, Cain would have never killed his brother. God did not make him do it, but God is accountable for making him human and giving him human nature. By giving us free choice, it is inevitable **WE WILL** make bad choices. If the only choice available was to make good choices, then it would not be a choice. That's all part of the human design, planned by God. All of our feelings, including jealousy, sparked by our emotions, are part of our DNA, designed by God, which makes God accountable for our bad choices, since it was God who put us all here in the first place.

When God gave us a choice, He is also including the possibility (permission, option) of bad choices. You can't just give your child the choice to eat broccoli or cookies and then punish them for choosing cookies, when you are the one who gave them the choice in the first place. God gives us the option to make bad choices and when we make the bad choice, He does not punish us. After all, He was the one who gave us the option to choose in the first place.

With that said, God did not give us free choice about everything. There are limitations. For instance, we had NO choice about being born in this human condition or thrown into God's plan of creation. He chose us. And, we had NO choice about who our parents are. If we had abusive parents or they abandoned us, we had NO choice about that either. Then, in order to cope with those abandonment issues, we become a serial killer. All because of circumstances we had no control over. God created the conditions in which we exist, and we did not have a choice. Not to mention, God did not give us a choice when He gave us free choice. So, when we make bad choices, God is accountable, because He set all this in motion. However, we are still responsible for our own actions, and we still have to incur the consequences that come with those actions.

God was well-aware of all this. After all, He was the one who designed us, and created us weaker than sin. He knew we **WOULD** make mistakes and we **WOULD** make bad choices and He was well pleased with His design. He said "behold, it was **VERY GOOD**". And, then He left us here with limited tools, so He **KNEW!** In fact, He expected it. It was intentional and part of His plan.

A common misunderstanding amongst a lot of Christian beliefs is they believe God made Adam and Eve perfect so they could live in this peaceful utopia with God indefinitely, but something went wrong, terribly wrong. God's original plan went side-ways and Adam totally messed things up for the rest of us, then Jesus had to come save the day. That is simply **NOT** true.

According to **I Peter 1:18-20 (ESV)** Jesus was slain before the foundation of the world, before creation even started. In other words, it was all part of God's plan, ahead of time, that Adam would mess up and Jesus would be the savior of the world.

It was never God's plan or intention that we live a sin-free life. Since God designed us, He knows our character and He knew Adam's nature and God **expected** him to mess up. It was just a matter of time. It was all part of God's plan. God was **NOT** disappointed with Adam because Adam reacted exactly the way he was supposed to...like a human.

Let's explore from God's point of view some of the possibilities of what He might have been thinking.

1. Let's say God did create Adam perfect with the intent of us living in some kind of utopia. What happened? Oh yeah, Adam messed up and blew it for the rest of us. **But wait!** How is that possible if God made him perfect? Did God make a mistake? Overlook something? Did God have an "Oh Crap" moment?

2. Let's say God did create Adam perfect but with free choice. Then, Adam made the wrong choice and blew it for the rest of us. **But wait!** If Adam

made the wrong choice, he still wasn't created perfect. You might be thinking that God started out with Adam Perfect but giving him free choice, expecting him to make the right choices, but Adam blew it. What are you saying? That God created us human, but He expects us to somehow rise above it and overcome our human nature and become something more than human, the same human nature that God created in the first place? That is like asking a cat to overcome her cat nature or a dog to overcome his dog nature. Our nature is inherent in us as it is in all creatures, whether cat, dog, snail, fly, seagull, or human. We cannot escape it. God designed us to be human with human nature. If God really intended for Adam to be perfect, then Adam would have been perfect, but he wasn't.

3. Let's say God designed us exactly the way we are... human, in this human condition, with human nature, weaker than sin. Then He gave us free choice so we can make bad choices and mistakes from time to time. God does **NOT** expect us to be anything more than that because that's exactly how He designed us. He knows we will make mistakes and He planned on us making bad choices.

Now, let's go back to what the Bible actually says. In **Genesis 1:31 (ESV)** after all the creation was finished, including man, God said "it was **very good**". So, when God created us human, weak, and easily over-powered by sin, He was still well pleased and said, "**it was very good".** Man must have come out exactly as God designed us to be.

All the evidence and scriptures point towards the third possibility that God intentionally designed us exactly the way we are, the way He intended us to be, including our capacity to make bad choices. Those four little words, that God said, keeps ringing in my ear, "**it was very good**"!

If it was Adam's fault, it was still God who created him and left him in charge, knowing how weak he was. And it was God who gave him the option to make bad choices. All of this still points back to God, that He created the conditions for Adam to fail and **it was all part of His plan**.

Now, let's elaborate a little bit more on God's plan, His intention, and His purpose when He created man. This is where people underestimate God, and they start to go down a different path from where the Bible takes you. We only have a few possibilities of how God set things up in the beginning.

God created this board game called "Life". Not the one you see at the toy store, but a life size version of that, where the board is a round object called earth and the game pieces are humans. Then, God created the rules.

First, you have the object of the game, then the general rules and then how to win.

Since we established that God is a planner, He's not going to leave anything to chance. So, as He was making up this game and the rules, He also had to plan the outcome of the game and how to win. God either...

1. **Planned on losing**. He created a game and a set of rules designed to lose. God made the game too difficult to win so that Satan and humans would eventually beat Him at His own game. Maybe God was not able to figure out how to create man, give him free choice, and still win the game.

2. **Or God is a loser**. This is where a lot of people underestimate God. They think God is a loser and He just can't keep up. And that Satan will join forces with a lot of humans and over-power Him. Then Satan wins the game when God gets fed up and sends whoever is left all to Hell. Satan will be laughing behind God's back.

3. **Or God plans on winning**. Remember, this is God's game and His rules. God considered all the pitfalls, all the obstacles, and He put us down here with Satan. Then He came up with an exit strategy that would guarantee He would win the game. After all, it is His game. He can take Satan out anytime He

wants or do anything else He wants in order to win the game. **God does not lose!**

Another misunderstanding is that a lot of people think God turned His entire plan over to mankind to make his own choices and direct his own path. Whereas **Jeremiah 10:23 (ESV)** says "it is not in man to direct his own steps". This is **NOT** man's plan or man's choices; this is about God and **HIS** plan. They forget who God is, who created us human with human nature, and who set this process up in the first place. And they forget who's plan it is and who is really in charge.

Remember this is God's game, not our game. God does not leave it up to humans to win the game. If He did that, humans would lose every time. And, as you can see, there are only a few possibilities of how God planned things out. Either God came up with a winning game plan or He intentionally plans on losing. Or He is a loser and He just can't keep up. However, as we explore further, you will see that God definitely has a winning game plan.

FREE CHOICE

*N*ow, let's circle back to free choice...
As I mentioned earlier, God does not control our actions. Some people call it "Free Will", some may say "Free Choice". But whatever you call it, it's that ability to make independent decisions and choices in life. It's not mentioned in the Bible, but it is clearly implied as part of who we are and our mental reality. It's all part of how God designed us.

Even though we have independent thought and free choice, there are limitations. For instance, God is not going to let our free choice disrupt **His free choice** to save the world. That is God's plan, God's choice. Even rejecting Jesus is not going to stop God from saving you anyway. All because that is God's decision, God's choice, God's overall plan. You cannot force God to change His plans just because **YOU** decided to go in a different direction. A perfect example of that is Jonah. He literally went in a different direction, but God still pursued him until His plan was complete.

Although some may argue that if we make the wrong choices, if we choose to reject Jesus, God will punish us. That is simply **NOT** true and **NOT** in the Bible! A choice means just that...a choice, which by definition is the option or permission to make good and bad choices. God gave us permission to choose either option. If your parents told you, when you were a kid, that you could walk to the store or they would drive you and you said, "I'm good, I'll just walk". Then they said, "Ok but it's 2 miles... each way and it's 92 degrees outside". You might come back and say, "I know, but I'll take my chances out there". Then you get back two hours later, exhausted and sun burned. Do they punish you for taking the difficult path? NO! After all, they are the ones who gave you permission to make the choice on your own. Just like God gave us the option to choose, on our own, whether to reject Him or not. He **DOES NOT** punish us because we happen to think rejecting Him is the right decision at that moment, based on our human reasoning. The same human reasoning God gave us in the first place.

When God gave us free choice, He is giving us permission to make both good and bad choices. Otherwise, if we were required to make the right choice every time, it would not be free choice. Besides, most of us feel like we are making the right choice at the time, based on our human reasoning. No one wakes up in the morning and says, "I think I'm gonna make a bad choice today". We are just reacting to our experiences and circumstances that brought us to that moment in life.

So, how are we supposed to know how to make right choices anyway? Especially when we didn't even get a choice about our circumstances or about being here in the first place. Not to mention, God designed us to have free choice without giving us a choice. It was all part of His plan.

We are the sum of how God designed us plus all these other experiences and circumstances, whether good or bad. The possibility of making a bad choice only exists because God included it in our design. He expects us to make bad choices, even planned on it. Besides, some of us may not even understand the differences between good and bad choices. For instance, the 9-11 terrorists believed they were doing good by attacking "Evil America". As mentioned earlier, we can kill, steal, worship Satan all we want, and God will not stop us. However, God did create the conditions in which we exist, and we did not get a choice and sometimes those conditions that God gave us takes us down a dark path.

Let's recap for a minute.

1. God made us human, after the God kind, but weak, easily over-powered by sin.

2. God was very pleased with the results.

3. God's expectation is that we act and react just like humans, as He designed us.

4. God gave us free choice knowing we will make bad choices.

5. If we did not make bad choices, we would not be human.

6. Since all roads lead back to God, then we have to consider that the capacity for making bad choices plays a part in God's plan as it relates to our development and human experience.

So, what am I trying to say here? All this crazy talk about being human and in the human condition. Basically, God designed us to look and act like humans with human nature and the capacity to do evil deeds. It was all part of God's plan. We were doomed from the beginning. Adam was already at a disadvantage. We never had a winning chance. And God planned it that way, so we would fail.

You might be thinking God didn't do that, He didn't make man that way. If God didn't do it, then who did? How in the world did man become that way and end up making a mess of things? Some say sin came into the world and made man that way. But the only way that is possible is if God made man weaker than sin. After all, it was God who designed us. Besides, sin was already here when God left us down here alone with sin.

Everything still boils down to God intentionally set all this in motion and He gave us the capacity to make bad choices. However, we still have to incur the consequences of those bad choices. But, if this was not God's plan, if He did not do all this intentionally, then the only other possibility is that God somehow made a mistake.

Let's take a detour for a minute and fast forward to **Romans 3:10–12 (ESV)** where Paul is talking to the Romans, both Jew & Gentiles, who believe in Christ. Prior to Jesus, the Jews were considered "God's people" and the physical evidence of that was circumcision. I wonder if the Jews, when entering the "club house", had to flash their junk to prove they were a member. In today's culture it would be a tattoo or something like that. I'm sure the Jews felt special, like they were important and had a special connection with God. Not only were they circumcised but they also had the law.

The Jews were like the firstborn child, but here comes the "new baby", the Gentiles, who were NOT circumcised. The Jews had a problem with that. They thought the Gentiles should get circumcised in order to become part of their clique. Paul was setting the record straight. He was explaining to them that neither circumcision nor uncircumcision has any value. The Jews and Gentiles are equal in God's eyes. In fact, Paul goes on to say in v10, "None is righteous, no, not one". Then, v11, he continues and says, "No one understands; **no one seeks for God**". Then in v12 he says, "No one does good, not even one". So, it does not matter if you are circumcised or not, **no one seeks for God.**

Then, we go to **Romans 3:23 (ESV)** where it says, "For all have sinned and fall short of the glory of God". Basically, after hearing this, Paul is saying we are all doomed. There is no value in doing good, we still fall short of the glory of God. We are equal to the serial killer, the child molester, and the Satan worshiper. No matter how much good **WE** "try" to do, we still fall short of the glory of God. There is nothing **WE** can do. It is too late! We are all lost.

After hearing this, what's the point of doing good? We still fall short of the glory of God, right? Well, there are a lot of reasons for doing good. Even though we didn't get a choice about being here, I think we have a responsibility to try to be the best humans we can possibly be. And, during our stay here, we have to interact with other humans who did not get a choice about being here either. Things will go a lot smoother if we can learn to get along and make things as pleasant as possible by treating each other right and being a good neighbor to each other, as much as possible. If we do not learn to get along with each other, it will be a very long and miserable ride. Although, this is all on a human level, because we have all sinned and fall short of the glory of God.

Then, after hearing all that bad news, Paul hits us with more bad news in **Romans 6:23 (ESV)** where he says, "The wages of sin is death". At this point, we have all **sinned** and fall short of the glory of God and now Paul tells us that **the wages of sin is death**. So basically, we are doomed, and we have a death sentence hanging over our heads. Great! Now what? Things are not looking good! So, in the meantime, we might as well make this existence as pleasant and peaceful as possible and treat each other with respect.

Wait a minute! That's not the end of the story. Let's go back to the Garden of Eden. God gave Adam one simple choice, but he couldn't handle it. And God knew that. After all, God designed him. God knows His product. He knows what he is capable of and what he is not.

So, do you ever wonder why God created humans this way, gullible and easily tricked, and then put us down here with a master trickster like Satan. God certainly could have locked Satan up before creating man, right. But instead, He left us down here with him. In fact, God is going to lock him up in the future. In **Revelations 20:1-3** it talks about locking Satan up for a thousand years, so we know God could have done it if He wanted to, but He didn't...Hmmm, interesting. It certainly seems like He did that intentionally. It must have been part of His plan.

So, let's get back to the Garden, to **Genesis 2:16-17 (ESV)**. This is where God told Adam that he could eat of every tree and all the fruit in the Garden in v16, but in v17 God says, "But of the tree of the knowledge of good and evil, you shall not eat of it: for in the day that you eat of it you shall surely die".

Now, I want you to notice something very interesting. God says "**in the day**" that you eat. Then, I looked at some other translations and found that some translations say **when you eat** of it you shall die. I don't see anything about "**if" you eat** of it. It is all about **in the day** you eat of it or **when you eat** of it, as if God was expecting it.

Then, God left Eve alone with the Serpent, knowing very well what was about to happen, and, sure enough, in **Genesis 3:6**, Adam and Eve ate the fruit and I bet it was good. Then, what came next was God giving Adam the third degree about what he'd done, and He was pointing out all the consequences. Not a punishment. Just consequences. God already told them what would happen if they ate of it. They would surely die, which is the end result of eating the fruit. Obviously, that was not an immediate drop dead you are gone kind of dead and it was not an implication that if they did not eat it that they would live forever. Adam was created mortal and it was never God's intention that he live forever as a human. Then what did God mean by "you shall surely die"? Well, we know they did not just drop dead. In fact, Adam lived to be 930 years old. The expression "surely die" was translated from the original Hebrew and it means to die over time. The exact translation is "dying you will die". And, throughout the Bible, the words Death or Die typically refer to a physical death.

A lot of people read the scriptures in **Genesis 3** following the eating of the fruit and think God was laying down his punishment. If I say to you, "if you jump off that 10-story building, you will die", that's not punishment. I'm just telling you the consequences of what will happen based on my limited knowledge of physics. And, since sin brings death and destruction, God is explaining what will happen. Besides, why would God punish them for acting like humans, when God created them human in the first place. Are they not supposed to do that...act like humans? There is no mention of a punishment, just that they would die. Since they did not follow the rules, God kicked them out of the Garden. There was no mention of going to Hell. If you steal money from your job, you get fired. That is not punishment, that's consequence. Going to jail would be punishment. And, if you tell your 18-year-old son that the house rules are no drinking and then he comes home drunk one night and you throw him out; that is not punishment that is promise. You kept your promise! You told him X = Y and he did X, so it should be no surprise his bags are already packed.

And for those who think God does not bless sinners, think again! We are all sinners and God still blesses us. Not because of what we do, but because of **who He is**. So, after everything is all said and done and God kicked Adam and Eve out of The Garden, God blessed them in **Genesis 3:21 (ESV)** with new clothes. They were naked and scared and all alone, so God had mercy and clothed them.

Now, after all this, in **Genesis 4**, Adam and Eve started to reproduce and they had Cain and Abel. Abel was a man of God and Cain was not. Cain eventually killed his brother Abel, so God sent him away in exile. He started his own village and started populating it. There is some evidence that Cain remained bitter over the years and the Cainites had become evil people. In fact, one of Cain's Great, Great, Great Grandchildren named Lamech also killed a man.

Then, as time went by, Adam and Eve had another son, named Seth, then Seth had a son named Enosh. And it was not until Enosh that man began to call upon the name of God, Two hundred and thirty-five years after Adam. Basically, we have Cain's people on one side, who strayed from God, and Seth's people through Enosh who followed God.

Then, when Enosh was 90, he had Kenan. When Kenan was 70, he had Mahalalel. When Mahalalel was 65, he had Jared. When Jared was 162, he had Enoch. Then, when Enoch was 65, he had Methuselah.

So, when Methuselah was born, it was Six hundred and eighty-seven years since creation. Then, Methuselah lived to be 969 years old. And, according to the Hebrew language, the name Methuselah means "**when he dies, judgment**". Then, when Methuselah was 187, he had Lamech. And, when Lamech was 182, he had Noah.

As time went by, legend would have it, the Cainites would intermarry with the other villages and eventually wickedness would spread across the land. Then, over 1,000 years after creation, Noah was born, a Godly man. He was one of Enosh's descendants and grandson of Methuselah. Then, when Noah was 500, it says in **Genesis 6:5 (ESV)** that "The Lord saw that the wickedness of man was great in the earth". In **Genesis 6:13**, God decided to destroy man and start over with Noah and his family. This was not punishment, it was just a decision that God made to start over, due to man's wickedness.

Now, notice something very interesting. Methuselah was 369 when Noah was born. Then in **Genesis 7:6 (ESV)** it says, "Noah was six hundred years old when the flood of waters came upon the earth". So, if you do the math, Methuselah would have been 969 years old, which is the age he died. Basically, he died just before the flood. Therefore, as his name says, "**when he dies, judgment**". He died and judgment came upon the earth by way of the flood. This tells us a lot. One, God planned on the flood at least a thousand years earlier. And, it was not an impulsive act of anger, it was all planned out ahead of time. It was all part of God's plan.

Also, notice this...God **DID NOT** blame man for his wickedness. He simply made an observation... "The Lord **SAW** that the wickedness of man was great in the earth". Besides, it was God Himself who initially set in motion the possibility that the wickedness of man would exist by the way He designed us. DO NOT misunderstand me! God **DID NOT** create man evil or create wickedness, but He did create a human vessel capable of evil deeds.

Not to mention, God **NEVER** said man became wicked or evil. He said, "the wickedness **of** man", which is the wickedness coming out **of** man. In other words, the wickedness **of** his deeds.

Where did all these people go? Did they go to Hell? NO! There was no mention of Hell, just that God decided to destroy them. That is straight forward, right there in the Bible...God simply decided to destroy man.

What happened to man that their wickedness was great in the earth? I mean, after Adam and Eve, what else went wrong and why did things go sideways? Well, man was separated from God, and you do not see a lot of involvement by God for many years. Basically, you give man free choice and leave him to his own devices, without God, man totally messes things up. This still boils down to choices God made. He made man, put him in this human condition with the capacity to do evil deeds, then God left him alone with Satan and gave him free choice. God has to incur the consequences for all that, He is accountable. But God knew what He was doing, and it was quite intentional.

Although, we do have free choice in life about our behavior, what we do or don't do along the way, we **DO NOT** have a choice about where our journey starts at birth and ends with death. And, when our free choice to reject God is in direct conflict with God's free choice to save us, God is going to implement His free choice regardless of what our choice is. Our free choices do not dictate or control God's overall plan. In other words, our free choices cannot force God to change His plan.

In the meantime, God sometimes makes a detour in the middle of our journey, without giving us a choice. God will shut us down, leave us with our back against the wall, and no alternatives. There are plenty of examples in the Bible to demonstrate this. For instance, what if Noah turned God down and said, "I'm good bro, I think I'm gonna chill on the beach, smoke my weed, and build a raft when the time comes". Then what? Is God going to scramble and go look for a replacement? NO! Noah was it, the only one available for the job. God did not ask Noah's permission or give him a choice, He **told** him. Noah did not have a choice. When God picks you, you do not get a choice.

For instance, in **Genesis 12:1 (ESV)**, God **told** Abraham to leave his country and then in v2 He said, "And I will make of you a great nation, and I will bless you and make your name great, so that you will be a blessing". God did not give him a choice or ask his permission. He told Abraham that He would make of him a great nation...period.

Then, in v3 God says, "I will bless those who bless you, and him who dishonors you I will curse, and **in you all the families of the earth shall be blessed**". Notice something interesting. In Abraham **ALL** families of the earth shall be blessed. **ALL means every one** of the earth, **ALL** the families shall be blessed. No one gets a choice. This was a promise from God. Do you trust God to keep His promises even to those who don't accept Him? A promise is a promise.

Now, we fast forward to v12-13 where Abraham pimps out his wife to save his own life, which is such a dumb ass thing to do. We've all done our share of dumb ass things and Abraham was no different. He acted just like a typical human. Did God punish him for being a dumb ass. NO! God blessed him. Whaaat! How can that be? Why did God bless him? It's not because of what he did, but because God promised him in v2, and a promise is a promise. You can see God blessing Abraham in v16 when Pharaoh treated him well, with sheep, and oxen, and he asses, and menservants, and maidservants, and she asses, and camels.

Moving forward to v17, we also see where God plagued Pharaoh and his house **because of Sarah**. Not because of what Abraham did or said, but because of Sarah. And why would God plague Pharaoh because of Sarah? I don't know. Pharoah thought she was available, so he did nothing wrong. Maybe it was a way to protect Sarah, because when Pharaoh found out, he became livid and threw them both out with all their stuff, including what he gave Abraham. So, did God punish Pharaoh for what Abraham did? NO! That was not punishment. Had

God not plagued him, he would not have gotten mad and thrown them both out.

Then, later in Abraham's life when he was 99, God told him that he would have a child. Interesting! I would be freaking out. God **told** him! It was all part of God's plan. He did not ask permission or give him a choice.

What about Jonah? God told him to go to Nineveh. Well, Jonah had some personal conflicts regarding Nineveh and refused to go. Did God say no problem, I will get someone else? No, God chased his ass down and put him in the belly of the fish for three days. Was that punishment...NO! God will do whatever it takes to persuade you. In the end, Jonah really did not get a choice. When God has a job for you, you are it.

Then, there was Samson, son of Manoah and his wife. Back in **Judges 13**, God was having some issues with the Philistines. They were messing with His "peeps", the Israelites. So, God wanted to "take them out". So instead of hiring a hitman, God had His Angel come to Manoah's wife, who was barren at the time, and told her she would have a son and his job will be to "take out" the Philistines. This was Samson's job before he was even born. He was going to be a hitman. Did he get a choice...NO!

Let's recap again.

1. God created us after the God kind.

2. God created us in this human condition with human nature.

3. God was very pleased with the results.

4. God **DID NOT** punish Adam, Cain, or man for any of the wickedness in the earth.

5. God **DID NOT** send any of them to Hell.

6. God **DID NOT** make us evil. He made a human vessel capable of evil deeds.

7. God has a purpose and a plan. He made us part of that plan and **DID NOT** give us a choice.

8. God gave us free choice but **DID NOT** give us a choice about having free choice.

So, back to Adam and Eve for a minute. God gave Adam one simple choice, but he could not handle it. God knows us so well, that when He put the tree of the knowledge of good and evil in the Garden, He knew Adam and Eve would eventually eat from it. He knew how persuasive Satan was and how gullible Eve was. In **Luke 12:7 (ESV)** it says, "even the hairs of your head are all numbered". So, if He knows every hair on our head and He knows our heart, He also knows how we will react to any situation. After all, God designed us. God knows his product and He knows what we are capable of and what we are not.

The idea that we have free choice or free will is a bit deceiving. Of course, we have independent thought, what we eat, what we wear, where we go on a day-to-day basis. However, there are still boundaries and procedures within an organized system. We cannot go outside the walls of God's plan. That is our cage, our boundaries already pre-determined before we were even created. It is a system and process God designed, that we have to operate within. It may feel like we are in charge because we have free choice, but our existence is all part of God's overall plan, His ultimate endgame. He has already decided how everything is going to work out. After all, it is God's plan. And in order for His plan to work, He has to be in control of everything. He does not leave anything to chance. He never fails. If God left it up to us and our free choices, we would blow it every time. In fact, we read that we have all sinned and fall short of the glory of God. That's exactly what happens when God leaves the choices up to us.

To demonstrate how much God is really in control, let's go to the Book of Job. This is where God pimps out Job to Satan and then to make things a little more interesting, God and Satan had a little side bet going on. Why would God do this? **One**, He is completely in control. **Two**, God knew Job so well that He knew Job would not waiver from his faith. God would not have taken the risk unless He was 100% sure He would not lose.

Early on in the book of **Job, chapter 1 (ESV)**, it describes how blameless Job was and how he was a Godly man. Then it describes his 10 children and how rich he was by describing his livestock. Then, in v6, we see all the Angels reporting to God. Satan was there as well.

This is very interesting! This tells me that Satan still has to report to God. He is completely under God's rule and control. Some people think Satan just went rogue and does whatever he wants. That is **NOT** true! God sees what Satan is doing and God limits his involvement or allows it at His discretion. He can stop Satan any time He wants, but it is all part of God's plan.

Then, in v7, God saw Satan standing there and said something to him like, "what you been up to, bro!". Then, Satan came back with some smart-ass answer, "going to and fro on the earth, and from walking up and down on it". Here is where God starts to pimp out Job. And, since Satan was walking around on the earth, He figured Satan probably noticed Job down there, so God says in v8 "Have you considered my servant Job?", "A blameless and upright man". God is setting Satan up and he is falling for it like a rookie. Satan is so predictable. And God knows exactly how to manipulate him.

Then, in v9-10, Satan comes back with attitude, something like, "yeah, right, of course he's blameless and upright, you have protected him and his household and made it easy for him, you have blessed his flocks and herds". Then in v11 comes the bet when Satan says something like, "I bet if you take away everything Job has, he will curse you". Then, in v12, God took his bet and turned Job over to Satan for a while.

Why did God risk everything with Job? With God, there is no risk. He controls everything, including what Satan does or does not do. He leaves nothing to chance. **God does not lose!** And, when it comes to God's purpose and His plan for us, we do not get a choice.

Now, you may be thinking, these examples are the way God used to be back in the day, but things are different now. We have free choice. Wait a minute! For everything to play out according to God's will, God's plan, God's purpose, He has to control the chess board. Take David for instance. Had he changed his mind at the last minute, Jesus would not have been born. God does not leave anything to chance. If God told David, it's up to you buddy, you decide if you want to be the king and the ancestor of Jesus, and David said, "no thanks, bro", then what? God would have to find someone to replace David as the ancestor of Jesus. That would have totally messed up God's plan. He already worked everything out with Ruth and then with David to pave the way for Jesus. None of them had a choice.

Then, years later, when the Angel of God came to Mary and told her she would give birth to the savior of the world. Did God give her a choice, NO! God has to maintain control of every detail, so everything works out the way **He planned it**.

Then there was Paul, who, before he was Paul, he was a Middle Eastern, anti-Christian terrorist. He was good at his job, very enthusiastic. God did not condemn him for killing Christians or punish him for it. Instead, God wanted him on His team. So, God convinced him to switch sides. Paul did not have a choice. If Paul said no, was God going to say, "that's fine, but if you change your mind, let me know". NO! God does not take no for an answer, He is relentless and extremely persistent. If He wants you on His team, He will stop at nothing until you are on His team. He knows how to convince you and persuade you, without forcing you against your will.

In the big picture, we have free choice regarding our behavior on a day-to-day basis, but regarding our role and our purpose in God's plan we do not get a choice. After all, it is God's plan. You can see this by all these examples in the Bible. And there are many more.

God created us human, and He created everything that makes us human including our capacity to make bad choices, really bad choices. Then, in spite of our human nature and our bad choices, God came up with a plan of salvation for everyone. If it is God's will, God's plan to save everyone, then everyone **WILL** be saved. You cannot escape God's will.

Then the question is: Did God intentionally create humans, with human nature, as part of His winning plan where He controls the outcome? Or did God plan to lose by leaving everything to chance, knowing the odds were against Him, or is He a loser?

Sometimes I think we forget who God is and who is in charge. I mean, did God create man, give him the capacity to make bad choices, then turn His plan of salvation over to man and expect him to make the right choice when making bad choices is all part of how God designed us in the first place? That doesn't make sense. In fact, as mentioned earlier, **Jeremiah 10:23 (ESV)** says "it is not in man to direct his own steps".

Let's recap once again.

1. God created us after the God kind, we are His babies

2. God made us human. He did not give us a choice.

3. God created us with human nature, and we make bad choices.

4. God was very pleased with the results.

5. God is in charge, and He has a plan and a purpose for all of us.

6. **God does not lose.**

THE UNTOLD TRUTH ABOUT SALVATION

A common belief amongst Christians is that those who Accept Jesus before they die will be saved and those who do not Accept Him will...well, let's just say it's not pretty. They will go to Hell, or they get burned up in the lake of fire. The Bible talks a lot about salvation but the idea of going to Hell or getting burned up in a lake of fire isn't making any sense.

1. Is God that weak that He can't figure out how to give man free choice and still save everyone? Does He not know how to convince everyone His way is the right way?

2. God knows us intimately. We've read that He knows every hair on our head. And He also knows our heart according to a lot of scriptures such as **Acts 15:8** and **Psalm 139:2**. He should know exactly

what it takes, what to say or do to show each of us His way is best. After all, He designed us.

3. Not to mention, the idea of Hell or a lake of fire means that God is going to lose a lot of souls to Satan. But we saw earlier in Job that God totally controls Satan, so how is that even possible. Is God a loser?

4. And, if God leaves it up to us to make those choices, it has been proven that we make bad choices. So, how can God trust us to make the right choice.

5. Besides, it doesn't matter anyway. We have all sinned and fall short of the glory of God. So, **Game Over!**

6. Game Over is right...for us and our bad choices. But **NOT** Game Over for God.

7. Then, considering that we are God's creation, made after the God kind, it does not make any sense that God would give up before He finishes the job. Is God a quitter? Is He going to abort His babies before they are born (again)?

8. Does God give up because we are too stubborn? Is He not able to mold us from a stubborn lump of

clay? If you physically die before being born (again), is God going to abandon you and spiritually abort you? NO! God can reach beyond the grave in order to rehabilitate you. In fact, that's exactly what He is going to do for those who died before knowing Jesus. He will raise them up in the resurrection so they can come to full term.

9. If everyone who dies without accepting Jesus goes to Hell (according to the common belief), then what happens when Satan is locked up for 1000 years, as we see in **Revelation 20**. Who is in charge of Hell? Wow! It's a free for all. That's when I take over.

None of this makes any sense, something seems to be missing. Things just aren't adding up. What does the Bible actually say?

We see in **Matthew 19:26 (ESV)**, where it says, "with God all things are possible". A lot of people have heard this scripture and it's been quoted quite a bit, but **the context** of that statement is overlooked most of the time.

If you start back in v16, Jesus is talking about the rich man asking what **he can do** to have eternal life. So, Jesus, being a smartass, in v17-21, told him what **he can do** to have eternal life. Then the rich man said no thanks and walked away. The emphasis was on what **he could do.** Whereas most people focus on v24 where it says, "it is easier for a camel to go through the eye of a needle than for a rich person to enter the kingdom of God", but it's not about the man being rich. It's about the man wanting to **do it himself**. The disciples knew what Jesus was talking about and realized it was impossible to **do it yourself** and in v25, they asked "**who then can be saved?**". Then Jesus answered in v26 and said, "**With man this is impossible**, but with God all things are possible".

There is nothing **WE** can do to be saved and get eternal life, absolutely nothing. Not even accepting Jesus or believing in Jesus can save you. You read it for yourself...**With man this is impossible**. It's a waste of time and energy to even try.

I know this is a big shocker. A lot of people have been taught "You have to accept Jesus to be saved" or "You have to believe in Jesus" But, we just read with man it is impossible to be saved. However, with God all things are possible. God is the only one who has the ability to save **ALL** of us, regardless of what we do or don't do. It is **NOT** up to us! **OUR** choices have absolutely nothing to do with salvation. God does not require us to do anything to qualify for salvation. Not even accepting Jesus or believing in Jesus can qualify you for salvation.

Then in **2 Peter 3:9 (ESV)** we see, "The Lord is not slow to fulfill his promise as some count slowness, but is patient toward you, **not wishing that any should perish, but that all should reach repentance.**" In this example, God **NOT WISHING** that any should perish is translated from Greek in other translations as **NOT WANTING**, **NOT WILLING**, or it's **NOT GOD's WILL** that any should perish.

So, if one of God's babies gets burned up in the lake of fire or goes to Hell, what does that tell us? It means that God was not able to fulfill His **WILL**. In other words, God failed, He is a loser. Isn't it God who is in charge and all powerful? Whatever is God's will, He gets! If God wants everyone to reach repentance, then "By God" everyone **WILL** reach repentance. God always gets His way. **You cannot escape God's will!** Not to mention, we just read that all things are possible with God when it comes to salvation.

Then there is the parable of the wandering sheep in **Matthew 18:10-14 (ESV)**, where the shepherd leaves the other sheep behind to go find the one sheep who wandered, just to save him. Here it is again in v14 "**it is not the will of my Father** who is in heaven that **one** of these little ones should perish". It is not God's will that even **one** person perishes. **This IS the will of God! You cannot escape it!**

Maybe you are thinking, since we have free choice, God **really** wants us to use our free choice to reach out and choose Him. Then, those who don't reach out will go to Hell. It sounds like **YOU** just decided, on God's behalf, that His will is that we reach out to Him. However, the Bible clearly says God's will is **that ALL should reach repentance, and no one should perish**. The Bible **NEVER** says we are saved if we reach out to Him. In fact, we just read that by man it is impossible to be saved.

Besides, how can we come to Jesus when the Bible clearly says in **John 6:44 (ESV)** that **"No one can come to me unless the Father who sent me draws them, and I will raise them up at the last day"**.

In this scripture the word "draws" was originally translated from a Greek word that means "drag". And, when it says the Father drags them, I do not see anyone getting a choice or that anyone will refuse to go. It simply says Jesus will raise them up in the last day...**ALL of them**, everyone who the Father drags.

In **Romans 6:23 (ESV)**, we read earlier that "the wages of sin is death". This is not a punishment. This is a promise. It's the price for sin. Wages are your earnings, your paycheck. If you take a job and they say you will earn $500 a week, then at the end of the week you expect to get $500, they promised. When you sin you earn death, that's your **WAGES,** your paycheck. God promised. However, with sin it is more of a reality of life that occurs automatically. Just like the example earlier... if you jump off a 10-story building, you will die. That is a reality of life. It has nothing to do with God punishing you to death. There is a law of physics that says for every action, there is an equal and opposite reaction. And for sin the equal and opposite reaction is death. God simply explains there is a price tag for sin, and it is death.

If you go to the store and get groceries, you are required to pay for them. Is that punishment because your kids are hungry and you need groceries? **NO!** It is the price for groceries. You cannot leave the store until you pay the price. And if you cannot afford them, someone has to pay. So, the guy behind you offers to pay and off you go.

Here is where things get a little dicey. You read the scripture above, right. **Romans 6:23 (ESV)**, "The wages of sin is death". There is no way to mis-interpret that or take it out of context...Death is Death. It is very clear and simple. The price for sin is **death**. Yet so many people say God really means Hell. But what they don't realize by saying God really means Hell is that they are unintentionally saying God is lying. Because there is no way to mis-interpret this scripture...Death means Death. In **Hebrew 6:18 (ESV)**, it says "it is impossible for God to lie". Besides, where do they get that idea of Hell in the first place? You cannot find any translation that interprets this scripture as Hell. Not even the original Greek text. So, where does Hell come in to play? We will look into that a little later, but for now, let's continue our thought.

As mentioned before, **Romans 3:23 (ESV)** says "For all have sinned and fall short of the glory of God". However, in **John 1:29 (ESV)** it says "Behold, the Lamb of God, who takes away the sin of the world!". That is great news! Jesus, who is often called the Lamb of God, took away the sins of the entire world; that is all sin in the world.

He paid the price for everyone...the world means world. And He did it without giving us a choice. We did not have a board meeting to discuss our options, He did not ask our opinion or take a vote. He just did it. It was part of His plan before He even created man.

Some may argue that Jesus only paid the price or took away the sins of those who accept Him, but that's **NOT** true and you can't find that anywhere in the Bible. You read it for yourself in **John 1:29 (ESV)**, He takes away the sin of the **WORLD**. That was God's choice not ours. Paying the price for everyone's sin has absolutely **NOTHING** to do with accepting Jesus. These are two completely different concepts. The Bible clearly says Jesus takes away the sin of the **WORLD**. And He did not give anyone a choice. **STOP**! Wait a minute! Think about that for a minute. Your brain may be saying "yeah, but...". However, nowhere in the Bible and I mean **NOWHERE** does it say there is a penalty for rejecting Jesus and not accepting Him as your savior.

It doesn't matter what you do to Him, whether you hate Him, curse Him, or spit in His face. He still made the choice to pay the price for **ALL** sin, including those who spit in His face. Why? Because it was decided long before man was created and long before anyone had a chance to reject Him. It was all part of the plan. A plan is a plan. And a promise is a promise.

You can also see that in **I John 2:2 (ESV)**, where it says, "He is the **propitiation** for our sins, and **not for ours only** but also for the sins of the whole world**". Who is John talking to when he says **not for our sins only**? Basically, he is saying that Jesus' sacrifice is not just for us who are already saved and born again, but it's also for the sins of the rest of the world. Besides, what does propitiation mean anyway? Well, it's another one of those Old English words. It basically means a sacrifice of atonement. And, as you can see, Jesus' sacrifice was for the entire world. This is very clear. Nowhere does it say His sacrifice is only for those who accept Him. There is no way to mis-interpret this. It says **"whole world"**. So, just like the guy who paid for your groceries, Jesus slips God $100 and off you go.

It's no different. You can't leave the store without paying for your groceries and you can't leave this world until someone pays for your sins. Since you can't' afford to pay the price, someone has to pay it for you. In fact, you are **NOT ALLOWED** to pay the price and you do not get a choice, it is already paid for you. Even if you try to pay by accepting Jesus or believing in Jesus, that is still not good enough. Besides, it is too late. The scales of justice are already in balance. The price has already been paid; the consequences of action vs reaction have already occurred.

Then we see in **I John 3:8 (ESV)** where it says "Whoever makes a practice of sinning is of the devil, for the devil has been sinning from the beginning. The reason the Son of God appeared was **to destroy the works of the devil**". This was the **REASON** Jesus appeared.

So, if Jesus came to destroy the works of the devil and sin is the works of the devil, then Jesus destroyed sin. Once sin was destroyed, you can't have a price for something that doesn't exist anymore. If just one man dies from sin or goes to Hell for sinning, then Jesus failed, since the **reason** He appeared was to destroy the works of the devil.

Since all have sinned and fall short of the glory of God and the wages of sin is death, then we **ALL** die, right. But Jesus came and paid the price for our sins, **not for ours only but also for the sins of the whole world** and He came **to destroy the works of the devil**. So, **we all live**. That is very clear in the Bible.

Basically, we either **ALL** die because we have all sinned or we **ALL** live because Jesus paid the price for the entire world. And if God really means the wages of sin is eternal life in Hell, then why didn't Jesus go to Hell for eternity in order to pay the price for our sins? Instead, He died, just like the Bible said...the wages of sin is **death**.

In addition, it says in **I Corinthians 15:25-26 (ESV)**, "For He must reign, till He has put all enemies under his feet." And in v26 "The last enemy that shall be destroyed is death." It **DOES NOT** say anywhere in the Bible that death is destroyed only for those who accept Jesus, it just says death shall be destroyed, period.

In **Hebrews 2:14 (ESV)** it says, "Since therefore the children share in flesh and blood, He himself likewise partook of the same things, that through death He might destroy the one who has the power of death, that is, the devil,". Basically, by Jesus' death, He not only paid the price for sin, which is death, but also destroyed sin, and in the process destroyed Satan, the one who has power over death, leaving **Satan powerless**. This is HUGE! Since Satan had the power over death and Hell, Jesus rendered him powerless, which means Satan does not have control over death and Hell anymore. So, who is running things down there, who's in charge, who took over?

It's time to recap again.

1. God created us after the God kind, we are God's babies.

2. God created us human, with the capacity to make good and bad choices.

3. God was very pleased with that.

4. Because we are human, we have made bad choices and we have all sinned. **Rom. 3:23**

5. This is all part of God's plan. He knew we would **ALL** sin. He designed us that way.

6. Because Jesus died, He paid the price for **ALL** sin in the world. **I John 2:2**

7. Jesus takes away the sin of the world. **John 1:29**. He paid the price for **ALL** sin.

8. God is in charge, and He has a plan and a purpose for **ALL** of us.

9. When God has a plan or purpose for us, we do not get a choice.

10. Jesus destroyed sin, leaving Satan powerless, so Satan has NO power over Death and Hell.

11. **God never loses.**

As we read earlier in **Romans 6:23 (ESV)** "For the wages of sin is death" but, if we continue reading that same scripture, it says "but, the free gift of God is eternal life in Jesus Christ our Lord". Eternal life is a free gift, unconditional, without giving us a choice and without requiring us to do anything. Just like we saw earlier, there is nothing **WE** can do to be saved or to receive eternal life. There is no qualification. Not even accepting Jesus can qualify us.

Since Jesus destroyed the works of the devil and paid the price for **ALL** sin, whether we accept Him or not, and eternal life is a **gift** from God, **then what's the point of accepting Jesus**?

First of all, notice something very interesting. We see many scriptures talking about Jesus as our savior, but **NOWHERE** in the Bible does it say that we need to accept Jesus as our savior or accept Jesus and you will be saved. I will say that again! The Bible **DOES NOT** say anywhere that we should accept Jesus as our savior or accept Jesus so we will be saved!!! Whaaat! How can that be? This is **NOT** Randy's idea or interpretation. Search your Bible and see for yourself.

However, the Bible does say those who **believe** in Jesus will be saved. It also says whoever believes has eternal life. For instance, **John 3:36 (ESV)** says, "Whoever believes in the Son has eternal life; whoever does not obey the Son shall not see life, but the wrath of God remains on him".

Two things I notice that are very interesting. First, it says whoever believes has eternal life. Basically, God is putting people into two groups, two teams. The first team is called "The Believers" and the second team is "The Unbelievers". The team of believers are those who are saved, **NOT** because **YOU** decided to join the team of believers, but because God picked you for the team. God is the team captain, so He can pick whoever He wants.

You can see that in **Ephesians 2:8 (ESV)**, where it says "For by grace you have been saved through faith. **And this is not your own doing**; it is the gift of God".

Believing in God **DOES NOT** save you. Although, those on the team of believers will be saved. Not because you decided to believe, but because God decided to put you on the team of believers. **This is not your own doing; it is the gift of God!**

Then we see in **Titus 3:4-8 (ESV)**, "But when the goodness and loving kindness of God our Savior appeared, v5 he saved us, **not because of works done by us in righteousness, but according to his own mercy**, by the washing of regeneration and renewal of the Holy Spirit, v6 whom he poured out on us richly through Jesus Christ our Savior, v7 so that being justified by his grace we might become heirs according to the hope of eternal life. v8 The saying is trustworthy, and I want you to insist on these things, so that those who have believed in God may be careful to devote themselves to good works".

Here we see in v8, those who believed, referring to this team of believers, God saved, not because they believed or any other works they did, but because of His mercy. Believing in Jesus **DOES NOT** save you!

Here is something else that's interesting in **John 3:36 (ESV)**. We see that whoever believes already has eternal life. It does not say **you will** have eternal life. it says you **have** eternal life. In other words, it's already determined. It's guaranteed. Then, those who do not obey shall not see life, but the wrath of God remains on him. What does that mean?

A lot of people assume if you don't see life that means death. If that was the case, then why didn't He just say that. Instead, it is the wrath of God that remains on those who do not obey or those who don't believe. This scripture says the believer has eternal life, but it **does not** say anything about the unbeliever seeing death or going to Hell. Besides, **NO WHERE** in the Bible does it say the wages of **not believing** is death. It says the wages of **SIN** is death. Although, it does say those who do not obey will **NOT** see life. That's not the same thing as death. Jesus already destroyed death. Since the believer has eternal life, those who do not obey or those who don't believe will **NOT** see life as in eternal life, but instead it's the wrath of God that remains on him.

In other words, the destiny of the unbeliever, those who do not obey, is the wrath of God. Death and Hell are already off the table since Jesus destroyed death and the works of Satan. As we saw several times, Jesus paid the price for **ALL** sin, for the entire world. So, what is the wrath of God anyway?

Since the word wrath means anger, people associate God's anger with human anger. A lot of people just **ASSUME** the wrath of God is where God gets fed up and blows a cork and goes ballistic. But that is another assumption. The Bible never says that. The wrath of God is nothing more than the name of an event that happens at the end time. It is **NOT** where God starts yelling and screaming and throwing stuff. It is just the name of the event, just like the rose bowl parade does not have a bunch of rose bowls parading around. It's just the name of the parade. We will look into this event called "wrath of God" a little later.

So, what is the point of accepting Jesus...oh I mean believing in Jesus? Especially, when He already paid the price for **ALL** sin and eternal life is a free gift. Just like it mentions in **John 3:36 (ESV)** above, it also tells you right there in **John 5:24 (ESV)** where it says, "Truly, truly, I say to you, whoever hears my word and believes him who sent me has eternal life. He does not come into judgment but has passed from death to life".

Once again, we see whoever believes already **has** eternal life. And, it says nothing about the unbeliever dying or going to Hell. It says whoever believes will not come into judgment. Since the team of believers will not come into judgment, then the unbelievers must come into judgment. Sounds like the event called "wrath of God" and "judgment" are either the same event or at least happens together at the same time.

Also, notice the phrasing. The Bible does not say "**if** you believe", it says "whoever believes". In other words, whoever is on the team of believers. If believing in Jesus saved you and if it was up to **YOU** to come to Jesus and believe, that would make believing in Jesus a qualification for salvation. It would be **YOU** doing it, by **YOUR** works, **YOUR** choices. And we read earlier that by man this is impossible.

Besides, everything we're seeing here in the Bible is God's plan, God's choices. And our free choice to believe or not to believe will not alter or control God's choice, God's plan to pay the price for **ALL** sin and save the **ENTIRE WORLD**.

Basically, for those who believe, those who are on the team of believers, God will automatically give you Eternal Life, a free gift, just like that...It's FREE! What about those who don't believe? Jesus already destroyed death and paid the price for **ALL** sin. They have no place to go. They are backed into a corner with no way out. But, according to the scriptures above, they will come to judgment and the wrath of God remains on them...**NOT** death or Hell!

According to what we've read so far, Jesus paid the price for **ALL** sin, for the **WHOLE WORLD**, for **EVERYONE,** so **NO ONE** will be required to pay the price or die for their sins. Then we see in **Hebrews 9:28 (ESV)**, "so Christ, having been offered once to bear the sins of many, will appear a second time, **not to deal with sin** but to save those who are eagerly waiting for him".

Basically, when Jesus returns, he's **NOT** dealing with sin anymore, sin has already been destroyed, he is **ONLY** bringing salvation...for those eagerly waiting. But what about the rest of the world? Jesus already paid the price for the entire world. And, since He is not dealing with sin it also means He won't be sentencing anyone to death or Hell. So, what does happen to the rest of the world? They have no place to go so they'll have to wait. Wait for what? It's not their turn yet. They have to wait for judgment and the wrath of God, as we saw earlier, while the believers, those eagerly waiting, will be saved.

Let's take a minute to think about something...

1. Jesus already paid the price for **ALL** sin, which is death (not Hell).

2. Jesus paying the price for **ALL** sin is a choice He made and it has absolutely **NOTHING** to do with whether we believe in Him or not. He made that choice before He created man.

3. Therefore, if you do not believe in Jesus, if you reject Him, He already paid the price for you anyway. Your rejection cannot undo that.

4. Then, in **Hebrews 9:28 (ESV)** it says when Jesus returns, he is **NOT** dealing with sin. He is only bringing salvation.

5. I may be getting ahead of myself, but later we will hear about those not found in the book of life being thrown into the "lake of fire". Many think this is Hell or burning alive for our sins, but that would contradict Hebrews where it says Jesus is not dealing with sin when He returns.

6. And, since Jesus is not dealing with sin when He returns, the "lake of fire" **CANNOT** be some kind of punishment for sin. It's symbolic of something, but definitely **NOT** Hell. We'll look into that later.

7. Some still think this may be a penalty for rejecting Jesus, but **NO WHERE** in the Bible does it mention a penalty or price for rejecting Jesus.

8. However, the Bible does clearly say whoever believes in Jesus is saved. What does that mean? And, **Saved from what?**

    a. As mentioned before, some think we are saved from death or Hell, but that's just an assumption and a direct contradiction from what the Bible clearly says.
    b. We already saw that Jesus paid the price for **ALL** sin, whether we believe in Him or not, so it can't be that. **Then what is it?**
    c. On one hand, the believers are already saved, and the death penalty has already been paid, even for the unbelievers. So, what happens to the unbelievers? They have nowhere to go, but yet eternal life is a free gift. Do they get eternal life anyway? **Yes!** Whaaat! How can that be?
    d. Eternal life is free for everyone...free is free!

e. The unbelievers will have eternal life because it's free, but not before first coming to judgment and seeing the wrath of God. And eventually they will repent. God said He will wait until **ALL** reach repentance. And, since death and Hell are off the table, they have no place to go. They are backed in a corner where the only option left is to repent and become a believer.
f. Now, if you are thinking, sure the unbeliever has eternal life...eternal life in Hell. That is simply **NOT TRUE** and **NOT** in the Bible. As we saw in **Romans 6:23 (ESV)** Paul was comparing the difference between the wages of sin, which equals death (not Hell) to eternal life when he said "**but**, the free gift of God is eternal life in Jesus Christ our Lord". Not only are these two different things, but eternal life is **in Jesus**, not in Hell.

Continuing our thought, the New Testament references some 50 plus scriptures talking about those who are saved. Saved by grace, confess with your mouth, those who believe in Jesus will be saved. **Saved from what?** Death? Hell? We already saw that Jesus destroyed the works of the devil and He destroyed death, so what is it we are being saved from?

Salvation is **NOT** about being saved from death or Hell as some may think. Take a minute to think about that. Does the Bible actually tell us what it is we are being saved from? Most of the 50 plus scriptures that mentions salvation never mentions **what we are being saved from**, so we just assume it means death or Hell.

However, it does tell us in **Romans 5:9 (ESV)** when Paul is talking to those already saved and he says, "Since, therefore, we have now been justified by his blood, much more shall we be saved by Him from the wrath of God". Those are the ones who are saved now (from the wrath of God) and everyone else, the unbelievers will endure the wrath of God. They will still see eternal life, it's free, but first they will go through the wrath of God. Death and Hell are not an option anymore. Jesus took the hit for that, so the unbelievers have no place to go.

And then Jesus mentions it in **John 5:24 (ESV)**, where He says "Truly, truly, I say to you, whoever hears my word and believes him who sent me has eternal life. He does not come into judgment but has passed from death to life".

These are the only two scriptures that I found that tells us what we are being saved from. On one hand, the believers are saved from the wrath of God, then Jesus said those who believe in Him who sent Him will **NOT** come into judgment. In other words, **saved from judgment**. Whereas judgment is not about punishment or sentencing. It is the process of finding out who is guilty. Basically, separating everyone into two different groups, two teams...the guilty and the not guilty.

Before you get all worked up and say...Ah Ha, there you go, judgment and the wrath of God, that's where they get thrown into Hell. It's **NOT!** It doesn't say anything about death or Hell. The wrath of God and Judgment are end time events in **Revelation**. It is **NOT** where God punishes all the unbelievers and throws them away like a piece of garbage. As you already saw, Jesus paid the price, so God is not going to make the unbelievers pay a second time when Jesus already paid the price the first time. Besides, we read that Jesus is **ONLY** bringing salvation when He returns.

Even Paul let it slip when he was writing to Timothy in **I Timothy 4:10 (ESV)** where he said, "we have our hope set on the living God, who is the **Savior of all people**, especially of those who believe". Whereas Jesus is the Savior of **ALL** people as we've seen in so many other scriptures. Here he says **especially** those who believe, meaning the believers come first, they take priority. Then there is the rest of "**ALL**" people... which are the unbelievers. They are a lower priority but still part of "**ALL**" people. If Paul meant **only** those who believe, he would have said that. But instead, he said **especially** those who believe.

9. So, when you read about all the end time events and those not in the book of life getting thrown into the lake of fire and all the drama of **Revelation**, it's all symbolic of the unbeliever going through the fiery trials referred to as the wrath of God. More about that later.

As we get further along, you will see all this explained and how it ties together with what we've already discovered.

As we can see in **Romans 10 (ESV)**, Paul is dealing with this argument between the Jews and the Gentiles. The big debate is who will be saved and who will not be saved. That argument is the same argument we see today amongst various religious groups. In v9, Paul clears that up and says, "if you confess with your mouth that Jesus is Lord and believe in your heart that God raised him from the dead, **you will be saved**". And that is period, regardless of whether you are a serial killer, child molester, etc. your actions and behavior has absolutely nothing to do with salvation. If you confess with your mouth and believe with your heart, **you will be saved**, period. Then, it says it again in v13, "everyone who calls on the name of the Lord **will be saved**". And as we saw above, they are saved from judgment and the wrath of God.

Don't misunderstand me. Just because your behavior has nothing to do with salvation, it doesn't mean it's an excuse to go out and start killing people. It's just that there is no requirement for salvation. It does not require you to stop killing or stop any other human related behavior. But you may want to change some bad behavior patterns on your own to avoid any messy consequences.

What is going to happen to all the people who don't confess with their mouth and believe with their heart? They have no place to go, death and Hell have already been destroyed. Are they going to say, "No thanks bro, I got this!"? Although, the common belief is that those people will go to Hell. However, they may have not heard that Jesus destroyed the works of the devil, but these are the same people who are saying that God doesn't have what it takes to reach everyone. Then, some may argue that is what free choice is all about. But we also see that we are not equipped to make the right choices. So, why would God create us without the right tools to make good choices, but then leave us hanging out there on our own and expect us to make the right choice regarding the biggest decision of our life.

So, when Paul said in **Romans 10:9 (ESV)** "if you confess with your mouth that Jesus is Lord and believe in your heart that God raised him from the dead, **you will**

be saved, that's only half the equation. He never said what would happen to those who don't confess with their mouth. However, Paul finishes his thought in **Philippians 2:10-11 (ESV)**, when he wrote in v10, **"that at the name of Jesus EVERY knee should bow** of those in heaven, and of those on earth," v11 **"and EVERY tongue confess that Jesus Christ is Lord**, to the glory of God the Father."

Now, that is powerful. On one hand, he is saying **if you confess** you will be saved and then he is also saying **EVERY** tongue **will confess**, that is every tongue as in **EVERYONE.** Right there in front of you, in your Bible. Yet, a lot of people still don't believe God. It doesn't happen all at the same time, but the Bible definitely says **EVERY tongue will confess**...eventually. God does everything in order.

Not only that, God swears by it all the way back in **Isaiah 45:22-23 (ESV)** where He says "Turn to me and be saved, all the ends of the earth! For I am God, and there is no other. V23 **By myself I have sworn**; from my mouth has gone out in righteousness a word that shall not return: '**To me every knee shall bow, every tongue shall swear allegiance.**'". Are you still going to deny God and what He is saying? Right there in the Bible, God is swearing by it that every knee will bow.

Once I went back and started to re-read some of these scriptures in the Bible, things are starting to make sense. The pieces are coming together. Things are beginning to add up.

Then, if we continue with what Jesus said in **John 6:37-39 (ESV)**, v37 "**ALL** that the Father gives me will come to me, and whoever comes to me I will never cast out. v38 For I have come down from heaven, not to do my own will but the will of him who sent me. v39 And, **this is the will of him who sent me**, that I should **lose nothing** of all that he has given me but raise it up on the last day". **God does not lose!**

In v37, you can see that whoever comes to Jesus, He will **never** cast out. However, according to the scriptures, it is **NOT** up to us to come to Jesus. It says right there in v44 "**No one can come to me unless the Father who sent me draws them**". It is not our choice; it's God's choice.

That is another powerful passage a lot of people just breeze right by. It's all about God and His will, mentioned in v39 as well as what we've read in previous scriptures. It's not about us and our choices, it's about God's choice, God's plan, predetermined long before He created man. All that God gives to Jesus will come to Him, that is everyone. No one will turn Him down. And the will of God is that Jesus will **LOSE NOTHING** and raise them up on the last day. **This is God's will and God never loses**! Let us take a look at **Ephesians 1:3-14 (ESV)**.

> "Blessed be the God and Father of our Lord Jesus Christ, who has blessed us in Christ with every spiritual blessing in the heavenly places, v4 even as **He chose us** in him before the foundation of

the world, that we should be holy and blameless before Him. In love v5 He predestined us for adoption to Himself as sons through Jesus Christ, **according to the purpose of His will**, v6 to the praise of His glorious grace, with which He has blessed us in the Beloved. v7 In Him we have redemption through His blood, the forgiveness of our trespasses, according to the riches of his grace, v8 which he lavished upon us, in all wisdom and insight v9 making known to us the **mystery of His will, according to His purpose**, which he set forth in Christ v10 as a **plan** for the fullness of time, **to unite all things in Him, things in heaven and things on earth"**.

v11 "In Him we have obtained an inheritance, having been predestined **according to the purpose of Him who works all things according to the counsel of His will**, v12 so that we who were the first to hope in Christ might be to the praise of his glory. v13 In Him you also, when you heard the word of truth, the gospel of your salvation, and believed in Him, were sealed with the promised Holy Spirit, v14 who is the **guarantee** of our inheritance until we acquire possession of it, to the praise of his glory".

If you notice in v4 it says, **He chose us**. Once again, showing how God is in charge and He already had a plan, long before we came along. And we were all part of that plan. We do not get to choose God, He chooses us. Then, in v5 it says, "**according to the purpose of His will**". This is God's plan, God's purpose, God's grace, and **God's Will**, NOT ours. Just like we saw in **2 Peter 3:9 (ESV)**, where it says, "**not wishing that any should perish, but that all should reach repentance**" That is **God's will** that **ALL** should reach repentance and He predestined us according to **His will**. Then in v9-10 it says, "making known to us the **mystery of His will according to His purpose**, which he set forth in Christ", v10 "as a plan for the fullness of time, **to unite all things in Him, things in heaven and things on earth**".

So, here is the best part and most people don't even realize it, but the Bible actually tells you right here that the **mystery of His will, of God's will** is to unite **ALL** things in heaven and on earth. This is God's purpose, God's plan, God's will, not ours. Our free choice to reject God does not control God or stop God from using His free choice to unite **ALL** things in heaven and earth. We do not cause God to change His plan, His choice. Besides, **ALL** means everything and everybody. So, there you have it, right in front of you, in your Bible, in black and white. Yet a lot of people still don't believe it. Is God lying?

Now, let's go to **John 3:16-18 (ESV)** where God so loved the world...you may already know this one.

But before we take a look at **John 3:16** with new eyes, remember in Romans: we have all sinned and fall short of the glory of God. Knowing that we have all sinned and we are all condemned, John gives them a glimmer of hope when he says in **John 3:16**, whoever believes in Him shall not perish, but have eternal life.

The word perish means to die. So, whoever believes in Him shall not die. Then, in v17 it says, "God did not send his Son into the world to condemn the world, but in order that the world might be saved through him". John is separating everyone into two groups, two teams. The team of believers will not perish and automatically advance to the finish line. Remember this is God's game. And one of His rules is that whoever is on the team of believers will finish first. Whereas the team of unbelievers will stay where they are. They won't be able to advance their position just yet. There is no punishment, just John explaining the rules.

If you are on the team of believers, you will not die, even if you are a serial killer, you will still have eternal life. That is good news for all of you who are serial killers. I know, that sounds crazy, but that is exactly what the Bible says…whoever believes in Him shall not die, period. It does not say anything about changing our behavior. But wait! Read it again. Jesus did not come to condemn the world, meaning He is not finger pointing or being judgy. Instead, He came to **save the world**. It says world.

That is the whole world, the entire world, everyone in the world. That is everybody.

Then we go to v18 where it says, "Whoever believes in him is not condemned, but whoever does not believe is condemned already, because he has not believed in the name of the only Son of God". This sounds like a contradiction. On one hand, Jesus did not come to condemn the world but to save it, but then John says if you do not believe you are already condemned.

Basically, before Jesus came around, we were already condemned, we were all guilty. But now that Jesus paid the price for the entire world, no one will be required to pay the price a second time. Yet, all of us are still grouped together and considered guilty. Then, John comes along and explains that those who believe in Jesus will be moved out of the guilty group and into the not guilty group. They will move to the front of the line and be on the team of believers. Whereas the remaining unbelievers, who were already condemned, will stay where they are at the back of the line and continue to be part of the guilty group for now. They will not be able to advance their position just yet. Jesus did not condemn them. He didn't have to; they were already condemned before Jesus came around.

At this point, John was explaining the rules and separating everyone into two teams. John **never** said whoever doesn't believe would die or go to Hell. He just said they were condemned already.

Go ahead and read it for yourself.

...John 3:16-18 (ESV)

v16 "For God so loved the world, that he gave his only Son, that whoever believes in him should not perish but have eternal life. v17 For God did not send his Son into the world to condemn the world, but in order that the world might be saved through him. v18 Whoever believes in him is not condemned, but whoever does not believe is condemned already, because he has not believed in the name of the only Son of God".

Now, let's go back to Romans briefly. This time to **Romans 5:18-19 (ESV)**. It says, v18 "Therefore, as one trespass led to condemnation for all men, so one act of righteousness leads to justification and life for **ALL** men. v19 For, as by the one man's disobedience the many were made sinners, so by the one man's obedience the many will be made righteous".

Once again, it says right here in the Bible that **ALL** people will be justified. By now, you can see and hear that God has a plan. We don't get a choice about our role in God's plan. It's His plan, His rules, His chess board, and He is completely in control of how His plan turns out. He does not just leave it up to us and our bad choices to make His plan happen. He does not leave anything to chance. Everything is well thought out. Humans are not equipped to make those kinds of high-level decisions. Just look at our history and see all the bad choices man has made. It is all part of the original design and plan that God created within us.

Here is an interesting thought. Since one trespass led to condemnation for all men, did we get a choice in that? Did God consult with us before He decided to include us in with Adam's choice. We weren't even there. This was part of God's plan, God's choice. Just like we read that God decided that one act of righteousness by Jesus would lead to justification and life for all men, for everyone. We didn't get a choice in that either. God did not ask us if we wanted to "opt out" of the justification feature of His plan.

In addition to all these other scriptures, we see **Titus 2:11 (ESV)**, which says "For the grace of God has appeared, bringing salvation for **ALL** people". Once again, we see salvation for **ALL** people. It does **NOT** say for **ALL** people who believe. It just says, "salvation for **ALL** people".

Now, you might be thinking you can always reject salvation or turn it down. You might say "thanks but no thanks, I'll take my chances in Hell…let's parrrrtay!". It's too late. Salvation is for **ALL** people as you can see above. Not to mention, the gift of God is eternal life, you can't just give it back, it's a gift. Jesus already paid the price. You cannot un-do His sacrifice.

In **2 Timothy 1:8-10 (ESV)** Paul writes, v8 "Therefore do not be ashamed of the testimony about our Lord, nor of me his prisoner, but share in suffering for the gospel by the power of God", v9 "who saved us and called us to a holy calling, **not because of our works but because of His own purpose and grace**, which He gave us in Christ Jesus **before the ages began**", v10 "and which now has been manifested through the appearing of our Savior Christ Jesus, who **abolished death** and brought life and immortality to light through the gospel".

The same theme throughout the Bible continues right there in **2 Timothy 1:9 (ESV)**, as mentioned above, where it says God **SAVED** us and **CALLED** us not because of anything we did or choices we made. It is all according to God's own purpose, which He gave us long before we were born. Did you read that? This is HUGE! God **SAVED** us before the ages began; before we were even born. We had no choice; we were not even born yet. It was all part of His master plan from the beginning, well planned out and orchestrated. Just like we didn't get a choice about being born human, God did not consult us about His overall master plan. God directs every detail to make His plan happen. He does not leave anything to chance. And you can see in v10 that Jesus **abolished death**, but the wages of sin is death. So, if death is abolished, then no one can die for their own sins.

In addition to all these scriptures above, we also know that God is rich in mercy! We are already dead to Him, due to our trespasses, but because He is rich in mercy, He saves us anyway, without giving us a choice. One of the problems with the idea that God will send some to Hell or a lake of fire is that God's mercy gets in the way. God cannot turn mercy on and off. It is engrained into His character. He can't stop being merciful towards sinners and those who reject Him.

The only way God could stop having mercy on us is if He stopped being God. **He doesn't get a choice!!!** Just like we don't get a choice about being human. I can't stop being Randy, you can't stop being you, and God can't stop being God. He came up with a plan to create humans, give them free choice and still found a way to give everyone Eternal Life. His entire being is rich in mercy! That's just part of who He is!

According to **Ephesians 2:4-5 (ESV)**, Paul says "But **God, being rich in mercy**, because of the great love with which he loved us, **even when we were dead in our trespasses**, made us alive together with Christ—by grace you have been saved". Grace meaning that God did us a favor. We didn't earn it or deserve it, and we certainly didn't do it ourselves. God just did it, made us alive without giving us a choice or requiring us to do anything.

As you can see, the good news is that Jesus paid the price for **ALL** sin, so no one will have to pay, even if we reject Him. In fact, no one can afford to pay the price. Since Jesus wanted to save the world and no one else could afford it, then it became His responsibility to do it for us, so He came up with a plan to save everyone, without our help. God is merciful, which is part of who He is. **God has no choice!** Just like we have human nature, God has God nature. Even though Eternal Life is for everyone, those who believe will be saved first. God does everything in order, which we will see later as we get into the section on **Revelation**. But for now, let's explore what it means to believe or not to believe.

TO BELIEVE OR NOT TO BELIEVE

We have read it many times that **ALL** have sinned and fall short of the glory of God. That sounds gloomy and hopeless. It is very discouraging. How do you recover from that? How do you get back in God's good graces? How do **YOU** redeem yourself? Some think if you just accept Jesus, you will be saved, but that is **NOT** true. We found out earlier that accepting Jesus is not even in the Bible. Then, some may say if accepting Jesus isn't what it takes, then certainly you have to believe in Jesus and you will be saved. However, believing in Jesus **DOES NOT** save you either! If accepting Jesus doesn't save you and believing in Jesus doesn't save you, then how do **YOU** redeem yourself? **YOU** can't!

We read in **Matthew 19:25-26 (ESV)**, when the disciples asked, "who then can be saved?" Jesus responded and said, "with man this is impossible". It is impossible to redeem yourself. No matter what we do, we still fall short of the glory of God. Even if you are the most devout Christian or the most faithful servant, believing in Jesus still **WON'T** get you into Heaven! And if you spend your entire life getting ready for this moment, it's still an exercise in futility. It's a waste of time and energy. You can hang out with believers, you can do what believers do, you can act like a believer, talk like a believer, **YOU** can even choose to believe, but if God did not pick you and put you on the team and make you a believer, then you're **NOT** really on the team of believers.

Let's say for instance, you want to try out for the NFL cheerleading squad. You've been practicing all your life. You were cheerleading captain in High School and then you joined the competition team in college and won National Champions two years in a row. You are good and you know it! This is the moment you've been waiting for. You've been telling yourself and your friends that you are guaranteed a spot on the team. "I am going to be a professional cheerleader", you say. You have no doubt, you know you are going to get drafted. Then the moment comes when you try out and you crushed it! Then you wait and you wait, then nothing. You're thinking maybe they have the wrong number, so you call to see what happened. Then they give you the bad news, you got beat out by the girl down the street. The one with the bad hair and hardly has any experience, not to mention she has adult braces. You're thinking "you gotta be kidding me! How can that be?"

This is also depicted in **Mathew 7:22-23 (ESV)**, where Jesus says "On that day many will say to me, 'Lord, Lord, did we not prophesy in your name, and cast out demons in your name, and do many mighty works in your name?' v23 And then will I declare to them, 'I never knew you; depart from me, you workers of lawlessness.'

These were people who hung out with Jesus, acted like believers, prophesied, and cast out demons like disciples, but in the end, Jesus did not pick them for the team. So, on that day, referring to the day the Kingdom of God is established, Jesus did not know them because they weren't on the team. They were boasting about the mighty works **THEY** did, but it has nothing to do with what **THEY** do or what **YOU** do! It's not about **YOU** believing in Jesus, it's about **JESUS** making you a believer!

In the Bible, it specifically says those who believe or whoever believes will be saved. So how can believing in Jesus **NOT** save you? Because it has nothing to do with **YOU** and what **YOU** believe or don't believe. The Bible **DOES NOT** say **IF YOU** believe you will be saved. It says "**those**" who believe, referring to those people who believe or "**whoever**" believes, referring to whoever is a believer or whoever is on the team of believers. Just like the case of the perplexed cheerleader, you are **NOT** a believer until God makes you a believer and picks you for the team. Your experience, your talent, **YOUR** choice to believe has **nothing** to do with it.

Let's take a look at what the Bible says. We'll start with **John 1:1-4 (ESV)**, where John takes us all the way back to creation. He says, "In the beginning was the Word, and the Word was with God, and the Word was

God. v2 He was in the beginning with God. v3 All things were made through him, and without him was not anything made that was made. v4 In him was life, and the life was the light of men.".

What John is doing here is introducing John the Baptist to the scene. But before he can do that, he had to explain who Jesus is and who He was so he could explain why he's introducing John the Baptist in the first place. Otherwise, the introduction would be uneventful.

Then in **John 1:6-8 (ESV)** comes the introduction, v6 "there was a man sent from God, whose name was John. v7, He came as a witness, to bear witness about the light, that **ALL** might **believe** through him. v8 He was not the light but came to bear witness about the light.

After the introduction of John the Baptist, John continues talking about Jesus in **John 1:9-13 (ESV)**, where he says "The true light, which gives light to **everyone**, was coming into the world. v10 He was in the world, and the world was made through him, yet the world did not know him. v11, He came to his own, and his own people did not receive him. v12 But to **ALL** who did receive him, who believed in his name, he gave the right to become children of God, v13 who were born, not of blood nor of the will of the flesh nor of the will of man, but of God".

Notice a couple things...

1. In v7, John came to bear witness about the light, that **ALL** might **believe**. All means **ALL**.

2. In v9, it says the true light gives light to everyone. That's **EVERYONE**!

3. The bible never gives us the option to refuse the light, reject it, or turn it down. It says, straight up, "the true light gives light to **everyone**". Whether you want it or not.

If you're thinking **yeah but** what about free choice. Sure, we have free choice about our behavior, but **NOWHERE** in the Bible does it say we have to accept Jesus. That's just an expression someone came up with and sometimes preachers will say it out loud. If they do, it is irresponsible, because people will believe it, but it is **NOT** in the Bible and it is **NOT** true!

Then continuing our thought, we see that Jesus' own people did not receive him, however all who did receive him, who believed in His Name, He gave them the right (authority) to become children of God.

Now on the one hand Jesus gives light to **everyone** and John the Baptist bears witness so **ALL** might believe, but on the other hand not everyone believed, especially His own people. Do we have a contradiction here? **NO!**

The Bible **never** contradicts itself, so there must be a logical explanation.

The question I have is, how did all those who received Him and believed in Him become believers? How did they get on the team? Did **they** make a choice to join the team and become a believer? **NO!** The Bible just refers to this group as "all who believe". It doesn't mention how they got there or how they became a believer. In v12, Jesus gave them, this group of believers, the authority to become children of God, born not of the will of man but **born of God**. It's not **OUR** will, **OUR** choice, what "**WE**" do or what "**WE**" believe. Those believers were born a believer when they were born again, by the **WILL of God**. It's not our choice to believe, it's God's choice to make us believers.

Then we see in **John 3:16-18 (ESV)**, John is talking about it in more detail. "For God so loved the world, that he gave his only Son, that whoever believes in him should not perish but have eternal life. v17 For God did not send his Son into the world to condemn the world, but in order that the world might be saved through him. v18 Whoever believes in him is not condemned, but whoever does not believe is condemned already, because he has not believed in the name of the only Son of God".

As you can see, it **DOES NOT** say **if you believe** you will not perish. It has nothing to do with **YOU**. In this set of scriptures all God is doing is separating people into two groups, two teams...the believers and the unbelievers.

He's explaining the difference between the two teams and whoever is on the team of believers will not perish.

As mentioned before, it has nothing to do with what we do, what we decide, or our choice to believe. Even Paul mentioned that in **Romans 9:15-18 (ESV),** quoting what God said to Moses, "For he says to Moses, "I will have mercy on whom I have mercy, and I will have compassion on whom I have compassion." v16 So then **it depends not on human will or exertion, but on God**, who has mercy. v17 For the Scripture says to Pharaoh, "For this very purpose I have raised you up, that I might show my power in you, and that my name might be proclaimed in all the earth." v18 So then he has mercy on whomever he wills, and he hardens whomever he wills".

Notice v17, God explains His purpose is that He might show His power and His name might be proclaimed in all the earth. What happens if God loses someone to sin or anyone goes to Hell. God would be marked a loser, He'd be ridiculed, He would lose respect. Instead of proclaiming Great is your name in all the earth we would be saying to God, loser is your name in all the earth. Not to mention, Satan would be laughing behind His back. But that won't be the case, God has a purpose and a plan to demonstrate His mercy and His greatness.

Besides, if it was up to us to redeem ourselves by choosing to believe, then it would be **OUR** name proclaimed in all the earth because "**WE**" did it, "**WE**" made that righteous choice, "**WE**" redeemed ourselves. Instead, it has nothing to do with **YOU** and what **YOU** believe or don't believe.

According to the Bible, it says **Jesus is OUR redeemer**!

Then we see in v18, God actually hardens whoever he wants. Even if the truth is obvious and Jesus is right in front of you, you won't see Him, you'll be blind if God has hardened your heart. You'll never see the truth or believe in Jesus until God opens your eyes and softens your heart. Wait! What about free choice? Does God force you against your will? **NO!** But God does soften hearts and harden hearts, He opens our eyes and He blinds us, all according to His will. Although, you still have free choice about your behavior.

In the end, it's really God who does all the work. Yes, we have free choice about our behavior, but it is God who changes our heart. In fact, it says in **Philippians 2:13 (ESV)**, "for it is God who **works in you**, both **to will and to work** for his good pleasure". For God's good pleasure!

For instance, let's say you get a job, but your boss says all you have to do is sit there and look good. He will do all the work for you. You still have free choice. You can get up and use the bathroom, go to lunch, talk on the phone, or play games on the computer when you want. But then one day you get bored and decide to send a report to your boss. He's going to ask why you did the report? Then he's going to tell you that he already did it. You just wasted your time. That's basically what God is telling us. He will do all the work. Anything we try to do to get to heaven is a waste of time and energy.

Remember we saw earlier that the Bible doesn't say how the believers got on the team of believers. In most scriptures that is true. It just mentions "those who believe" or "whoever believes". It doesn't say how they got there or how they became a believer, but John explains in **I John 5:1 (ESV)**, "Everyone who believes that Jesus is the Christ has been born of God".

What does that tell us? It says that everyone who believes has already been born again. In other words, you must be born again first before you can become a believer. Anyone who claims they just randomly believed on their own and then came to God and asked Him if they could be born again, is not a true believer. Once you are born again, you will automatically become a believer and put on the team of believers.

And, according to God's mercy **He causes** us to be born again. And only by **God's will** can we be born again. **WE** don't choose to be born again and **WE** don't choose to be on His team, He chooses us. It's not our choice to believe, it's God's choice to make us believers by **causing** us to be born again. You can see that in **I Peter 1:3 (ESV)** where Peter says, "Blessed be the God and Father of our Lord Jesus Christ! **According to his great mercy**, he has **caused us to be born again** to a living hope through the resurrection of Jesus Christ from the dead".

Just like Jesus says in **John 5:38 (ESV)**, "you do not have his word abiding in you, for you do not believe the one whom he has sent". You can't just wake up one morning and say, "What a beautiful morning, I think I'm going to start believing today". First, His word has to be abiding in you. How do you get His word abiding in you? Is there a patch you can get to soak in the word through your skin? Can you have it surgically implanted? **NO!** Someone has to put it there. And, since you have to be born again first before you can believe and those who do not believe don't have the word abiding in them, then you must also be born again before you can have the word abiding in you.

In addition to all that, Jesus says in **John 6:27-29 (ESV)** "Do not work for the food that perishes, but for the food that endures to eternal life, which the Son of Man will give to you. For on him God the Father has set his seal." v28 Then they said to him, "What must we do, to be doing the works of God?" v29 Jesus answered them, "This is the work of God, that you believe in him whom he has sent".

Here we see we don't have to do anything, because it is **Jesus who gives** the food that endures to eternal life, but they still asked what **THEY** could do themselves. What Jesus answered back was **HUGE!** Basically, He said there is nothing you can do, **THIS IS** the work of God that you believe. So, it's not up to us to choose to believe, it is up to God to make us a believer. It is the work of God. That is His job!

Are you having another "**yeah, but**" moment? It's right there in the Bible. **THIS IS** the work of God that you believe. That is His job. Eventually every tongue will confess, and every knee will bow, but if anyone stays on the team of unbelievers, then God failed at His job. There is nothing **YOU** can do. If God wants to make you a believer, you will be a believer. I know it sounds like God is forcing us against our will, but He's NOT! It is **HIS** plan to save the world. Whatever God decides to do, **HE** will do! We have no choice. God already had His plan in place before He created man. This is God's game, His rules. He can make changes along the way to reach His end game. He can blind us or open our eyes, soften our hearts or harden our hearts as it fits together to make His plan work.

Besides, if it was up to our free choice, then our free choice would control God's free choice to finish what He started. And God is not going to let our free choice get in the way of Him finishing His plan and saving the **WORLD**.

There was a time when people understood this concept. Remember the old song Amazing Grace... "Once I was blind, but now I see". The writer understood it was by God's Amazing Grace that his eyes were opened. We can't heal our own eyes and suddenly see the light. And once God opens our eyes, we don't scream out "No God, blind me again". It is God who does all the work, who changes our heart, changes our will, heals our eyes, and **causes** us to be born again. When you read the message in **Jeremiah 18– 19 (ESV)** where God says He is the potter and we are the clay, what does the clay do? Nothing! The clay has no control over how God molds us or what God does in our lives or our hearts.

Basically...

1. God **CAUSES** us to be born again. **I Peter 1:3 (ESV)**.

2. You must be born again, **caused** by God, to be on the team of believers. **I John 5:1 (ESV)**.

3. You cannot believe unless you have the word of God abiding in you. **John 5:38 (ESV)**.

4. The only way to have the word abiding (living) in you is if God puts it there.

5. And it is God's job that you believe in Him who He sent. Not your job. **John 6:29 (ESV)**.

6. If anyone does not eventually believe, then God loses. He failed at His job.

WHO WILL INHERIT THE KINGDOM OF GOD?

We just found out that it is God's job that we believe and not our job. And we cannot believe unless we are born again, which is caused by God. If God does all the work, then what do **WE** need to do to inherit the Kingdom of God? And who else will inherit the Kingdom of God?

Remember, everything stops and starts with God. It was God who created man and put us down here to co-exist with Satan. And it was God who put sin at our fingertips. It was also God who gave us free choice so we can choose to reach out and touch sin. Giving us the option to touch sin was still part of God's plan. And it was God who had a plan in the first place before He created man. He wasn't just making this stuff up as He goes along. He had a well-orchestrated, well thought out and organized plan, which included leaving us down here with Satan.

First, God made man after the God kind. We are called sons of God, brothers, and sisters in Jesus. God created the birthing process to reproduce humans. Then, He told us about a birthing process to become spiritually born referred to as "born again". God is reproducing Himself! We have no control over the birthing process whether physical or spiritual. It's God's design, God's plan. We cannot choose to be born.

And we were just looking at **I Peter 1:3 (ESV)** where it says, "**According to his great mercy**, he has **caused us to be born again**". But then, if we continue in v4, we see that it says, "to an inheritance that is imperishable". Here we see God **caused** us to be born again to an inheritance. An inheritance to what? Was that our choice, our decision? **NO!** God **caused** us to be born to an inheritance. Did we have to qualify to be born again by believing in Him first? **NO!** God caused us to be born again. Besides, we saw earlier that all those who believe have already been born again, so we can't believe until we are first born again.

We also see Paul talking about it in **Galatians 4:4-7 (ESV)**, "But when the fullness of time had come, God sent forth his Son, born of woman, born under the law, v5 to **redeem** those who were under the law, so that we might receive adoption as sons. v6 And, because you are sons, God has sent the Spirit of his Son into our hearts, crying, "Abba! Father!" v7 So you are no longer a slave, but a son, and if a son, then an **heir** through God".

Here we see that God sent His son, who was born **under the law**, to **redeem** us so we can be adopted into the God family and now that we are in the God family, He sends His spirit, the Holy Spirit into our hearts. Being adopted into the God family, we are also heirs to the family fortune, heirs to the Kingdom. This was all God, **WE** had nothing to do with it. God sent His son to redeem us, so we might receive adoption. It was God who sent His spirit into our hearts, and it was God who made us heirs.

Take a close look at v5 for a minute. First, we saw in v4 that Jesus was born **under the law**, then in v5, God sent His son to redeem **those who are under the law**. Who are they, those who were under the law? Everyone is under the law! That means all of us. So, Jesus came to redeem everyone.

Also, think about something else for a minute. Everything God has done up to this moment has been intentional. God has been very deliberate. He came up with a plan of salvation for mankind long before He even created man. God is not making this stuff up as He goes along.

Everything we do in life is either intentional or by accident / mistake. When you boil it down, these are the only two reasons why we do anything, no matter who you are, including God. Even an emotional reaction is still an intentional act.

For instance, Cain killing Abel was intentional. Even though it happened in the heat of the moment and Cain reacted emotionally, emotions that God gave him, he still intentionally picked up the rock and hit Abel with it. If it was an accident, Cain would have been running towards Abel, tripped over his sandals, bumped into Abel, and accidentally pushed him to the ground and he hit his head on a rock. Either God created man intentionally too weak to avoid sin and then put us down here with Satan. Or God created man perfect, stronger than sin, but then Satan found a flaw in God's plan and this whole thing spiraled out of control and it turned out to be a big mistake. Then, God has been trying to fix things ever since. No, this was no mistake, no accident, this **WAS** God's plan from the beginning. He intentionally created man too weak to avoid sin.

Since God had a plan and everything is going according to that plan, then who did God plan on inheriting the Kingdom of God?

Earlier we established that **NOWHERE** in the Bible does it say we have to accept Jesus to be saved and believing does **NOT** save you either. In fact, there is **NOTHING** you can do to redeem yourself, to receive salvation. **YOUR** effort, **YOUR** choices do not get you any closer to salvation than you were before. Only God can save you. Eternal life is a gift, it's free. If you are thinking **YOU** chose God and **YOU** decided to believe, then basically, you are saved by your own choices. In other words, **YOU** did it, **YOU** reached out to God. Then why do you need God in the first place? You made it to Heaven on your own. By your strength to endure, you did it yourself, you qualified, **YOU** made it by choosing to believe.

However, it is not up to you. Just like it says in **Titus 3:5 (ESV)** "he saved us, not because of works done by us in righteousness" Besides, you can't really come to Him anyway. Jesus clearly says in the Bible that **NO ONE** can come to Him unless the Father drags them.

So, if only God can give you salvation and **believing** doesn't do it, then who is it that will inherit the Kingdom of God? Well, Jesus tells Nicodemus in **John 3:3 (ESV)**, "Truly, truly, I say to you, unless one is born again, he cannot see the kingdom of God." Then, when Nicodemus says Whaaat?, Jesus came back in v5-6 and said "Truly, truly, I say to you, unless one is born of water and the Spirit, he cannot enter the kingdom of God. That which is born of the flesh is flesh, and that which is born of the Spirit is spirit".

Well, there you have it! You must be born again, born of the spirit to enter the Kingdom of God. And the only way to be born again is if God **causes** you to be born again. It has absolutely nothing to do with whether **WE** believe or don't believe. It has everything to do with God putting His spirit into our hearts, **causing** us to be born again, without giving us a choice. Do **YOU** have to do something so God will pick you? **NO!** It is completely up to God. It is His choice. In **Romans 9:15 (ESV)** God says, "I will have mercy on whom I have mercy". In other words, those who God **causes** to be born again, those who God chooses, according to His mercy, **will inherit the Kingdom of God**.

Basically...

1. Once God **causes** us to be born again and He **makes** us a son of God, He sends the spirit of His son, which is the Holy Spirit, into our hearts. **Galatians 4:6 (ESV)**.

2. The Holy Spirit is a free gift to those who turn towards God. **Act 2:38 (ESV), Acts (10:45) (ESV)**.

3. Then, once we are sons, we become heirs through God. **Galatians 4:7 (ESV)**.

4. Once we are born again, we become believers, and then we are sealed with the Holy Spirit as a down payment and a guarantee of our inheritance. **Ephesian 1:13-14 (ESV)**.

Not only all that, but we just saw in **Galatians 4:4-5 (ESV)**, where Paul says, "God sent his Son to **redeem those who were under the law**". We cannot redeem ourselves. It is God who causes us to be born again and puts His spirit into our hearts which makes us heirs, without giving us a choice. And as heirs, we will inherit the Kingdom of God. There is nothing **YOU** can do. This is all according to God's plan. And what is that plan? Well, we read earlier that the **mystery of His plan** is to unite **ALL** things in heaven and earth. **ALL** means everyone!

However, God has a process and He does everything in order. First, He creates light, then He separated the water from the land, and so on. Then God created man on the 6th day, **all in order**.

Then if we go all the way back to **Exodus 23 (ESV)**, long before Jesus came around, God introduced the idea of the various harvest throughout the year. There was the first of the first fruits, then the first fruits and finally the harvest of the ingathering, which is the rest of the crop. All these things were in a particular order...step by step as God planned it. God is orderly. Later we will see that there are two resurrections...technically three if you count Jesus. Basically, the first of the first fruits represents Jesus. Then the first fruits, those who follow Jesus, and then the rest of the people.

You can see this principle of the first fruits and how God does everything in order explained in **I Corinthians 15:20-23 (ESV)**, where it says v20 "But in fact Christ has been raised from the dead, the **first fruits** of those who have fallen asleep. v21 For, as by a man came death, by a man has come also the resurrection of the dead. v22 For as in Adam all die, so also **in Christ shall all be made alive**. v23 But, **each in his own order**: Christ the first fruits, then at his coming those who belong to Christ".

This is very clear! **All shall be made alive**, but each in his own order. Very interesting. Another one of those scriptures that people seem to ignore. If it was up to us and **OUR** choice to believe, **NO ONE** would inherit the Kingdom. But it's not up to us, there is nothing **WE** can do. It is completely up to God. And God came up with a plan, a way He could save His entire family from destruction, to unite **ALL** things in heaven and earth. Every single one of us, **each in his own order**.

So, basically, the question is not about "**IF**" you make it to Heaven, it's about "**WHEN**" you make it to Heaven. We've read that **ALL** shall be made alive, and God will unite **ALL** things in heaven and earth...**each in his own order**.

We also see that James mentioned the first fruits in **James 1:17-18 (ESV)**. "Every good gift and every perfect gift is from above, coming down from the Father of lights, with whom there is no variation or shadow due to change. v18 Of **his own will** he brought us forth by the word of truth, that we should be a **kind of first fruits** of his creatures".

You can see in v18, Of **His own will**, God's own will that we should be a **kind of first fruits**. Not **OUR** will or **OUR** choices. And, just like Jesus was the first of the first fruits and then those who belong to Christ would follow. Then, if those who belong to Christ are a **kind of first fruits** as mentioned in **James** above, then the rest of the crop must come later. **Each in his own order**.

The Bible is very clear when it says, **"in Christ all shall be made alive"**. If all shall be made alive, then why does the Bible talk about those who will **NOT** inherit the Kingdom of God. Is this a contradiction? **NO!** Remember the Bible does not contradict itself. Let's see what the Bible says about all that.

In **I Corinthians 6:9-11 (ESV)**, some of the members of the Church of Corinth were suing each other over various disputes and grievances. Paul asked why they were taking their grievances to the courts of the world, who were the unrighteous, the unbeliever, those who have not been born again, and then he suggested they resolve their disputes within the Church, amongst those who were the saints.

Paul writes in **v9-11 (ESV)**, "do you not know that the **unrighteous will not inherit the kingdom of God**? Do not be deceived: neither the sexually immoral, nor idolaters, nor adulterers, nor men who practice homosexuality, v10 nor thieves, nor the greedy, nor drunkards, nor revilers, nor swindlers will inherit the kingdom of God. v11 And, such were some of you. But you were washed, you were sanctified, you were justified in the name of the Lord Jesus Christ and by the Spirit of our God".

Here we see that the unrighteous will not inherit the Kingdom of God, along with a laundry list of other things that will not inherit the Kingdom of God. Who are these people? Are they evil? Are they so far gone that they won't be able to inherit the Kingdom of God? NO!

Nobody is too far gone for God. Then who is Paul talking about? Who are these unrighteous people?

Well, according to Jesus, the only way to get to the Kingdom of God is by being born again. So, technically anyone who has not been born again are those who are the unrighteous. Whereas those who have been born again, are guaranteed a spot in the Kingdom. Even if you are a thief, a drunkard, a swindler, or anything else on that list, but you have been born again, **you are still guaranteed a spot in the Kingdom**. Whaaat! How can that be? Didn't Paul just say they will not inherit the Kingdom of God? Yes, but Jesus said those who have been born again will receive the holy spirit as a down payment, a **guarantee** that they will be in the Kingdom. That sounds like a contradiction, but it's not! We already know that God is **NOT** going to have any shenanigans in His Kingdom, so it is His responsibility to cleanse those who are unrighteous before they get to the Kingdom.

We also saw above that Paul had reminded the Corinthians that some of them where just like those on the list as well. So, what happened? Well, they were born again. They were washed in the name and blood of Jesus and by the Spirit of God. Did they have to prove themselves first, did they have to overcome or believe in Jesus before God would agree to cleanse them? Did they have to qualify? **NO!** Paul simply says they were washed in the name and blood of Jesus.

Since God washed and cleansed the church of Corinth, then He certainly can wash and cleanse the unrighteous... **each in his own order**. Can the unrighteous make themselves righteous? Can we cleanse ourselves? NO! That is God's responsibility. He **causes** us to be born again.

We've seen how God separates everyone into two groups: the guilty, the not guilty, the believer, the unbeliever, the first resurrection, the second resurrection, and now the righteous and the unrighteous. So, going back to **I Corinthians 15:22-23 (ESV)**, it is **VERY CLEAR** when Paul says "For as in Adam all die, so also **in Christ shall all be made alive**. v23 But, **each in his own order**"

The unrighteous are part of the other team who stays behind and has to wait until the second resurrection. When God says **ALL** shall be made alive, He means what He says.

It is God's responsibility, His job to cleanse us of our unrighteousness. Once we are born again and God cleanses us by the spirit, by the blood of Jesus, we will be good to go. Each in his own order. As for the unrighteous that Paul mentioned, it just isn't their time yet.

We also see in **I Corinthians 15:50 (ESV)**, where it says, "**flesh and blood cannot inherit the kingdom of God**". Not only will the unrighteous and all these evil deeds **NOT** inherit the Kingdom of God, but neither will any human, flesh and blood. Great! Now What? That's discouraging! Then why do we keep killing ourselves trying? We are all flesh and blood, right? So, none of us get to go? What a waste of time!

That's what I've been trying to say. There is nothing **WE** can do since we are all flesh and blood. Believing is not going to do it! We have to be born again! And it is God who **causes** us to be born again and it is God who cleanses us by the blood of Jesus, who also gives us the Holy Spirit, and then He transforms us from human to spirit.

We also see Paul talking to the Church of Galatia about walking by the spirit. In **Galatians 5:16 (ESV)**, Paul writes, "walk by the Spirit, and you will not gratify the desires of the flesh". So how do we do that?

Paul never tells us how to do that. Can we just close our eyes and squeeze really hard and then we will jump out of our physical form into our spiritual form? NO! So how do we walk by the spirit? **We Can't!** It's impossible to walk by the spirit. However, once God causes us to be born again and He puts His spirit into our hearts, we automatically "walk by the Spirit".

Then in contrast to v16 Paul continues in **Galatians 5:19-21 (ESV)** where he says, "the works of the flesh are evident: sexual immorality, impurity, sensuality, v20 idolatry, sorcery, enmity, strife, jealousy, fits of anger, rivalries, dissensions, divisions, v21 envy, drunkenness, orgies, and things like these. I warn you, as I warned you before, that those who do such things will not inherit the kingdom of God".

Here we see that Paul is demonstrating the difference between walking by the spirit and the works of flesh. He says, those who do such things, the works of the flesh will **NOT** inherit the Kingdom of God. We read earlier that flesh and blood cannot inherit the Kingdom of God and now we see that neither can the works of the flesh.

Does that mean if you slip up and get drunk, even though you've been born again, you lost your chance and you have to go back to the other team? NO! We read earlier that God gives you the Holy Spirit to guarantee you will inherit the Kingdom of God. That is His promise! So, if you can go on a killing spree, go on a three-day bender, cuss people everywhere you go, or worship Satan you **WILL STILL** inherit the Kingdom of God. Whaaat! How can that be? God promised! And a promise is a promise.

We have free choice, but regardless of what we do, we will never make God change His plans or His promises. If we turn around and start worshiping Satan at the last minute, we still get to mosey on into the Kingdom, God guaranteed our spot in the Kingdom. And God is a man of His word!

However, when God causes us to be born again and gives us the Holy Spirit, He gives us a new heart. Therefore, we don't want to do these things anymore. That's what Paul is talking about when he says, "walking by the spirit". Besides, it is not up to us to overcome the works of the flesh. That is God's job, God's responsibility to change us from flesh to spirit.

However, those who are **NOT** born again are still on the other team that continues to practice the works of the flesh. Therefore, **God has decided not** to cleanse them yet or cause them to be born again. **NOT** because He's waiting for them to decide, but because He decided to wait. It's not their time yet. God does everything in order.

1. So, who will inherit the Kingdom of God? Those who are born again.

2. How do you become born again? It's the works of God. He causes us to be born again.

3. God sends His spirit into our hearts.

4. Who will be saved? Those who believe.

5. How do you become a believer? Also, the works of God. The believers are those who have been born again, caused by God.

6. We read it was impossible for man to be saved, but by God all things are possible.

7. We cannot redeem ourselves, so it's up to God to do all the work.

8. Flesh and blood will **NOT** inherit the Kingdom of God. And neither will the works of the flesh.

9. In Adam **ALL** die, but in Jesus **ALL** shall be made alive.

10. So, who will inherit the Kingdom of God? Everyone, according to God's plan. It's a gift! A promise! **Each in his own order**.

We've learned a lot about salvation and what it means to believe. And we've discussed who will inherit the Kingdom of God. I know a lot of this is new and it contradicts what we've been taught or heard most of our life. But the scriptures are clear. They are right there in black and white when you look at the big picture. If you go back and re-read these scriptures on your own and think about how it all relates to God's plan, the pieces will start to come together.

With all this new information we're seeing, it gives us pause to re-think some old ideas. And, with a whole new outlook on salvation and what it means to believe, it makes me wonder what really happens when we die and what about Hell? As we explore the Biblical evidence around these questions, things will start making a lot more sense.

WHAT REALLY HAPPENS WHEN WE DIE?

Since Death and Hell have been abolished by Jesus and He destroyed sin along with the works of the devil, and Satan was left powerless, let's take a minute to talk about what happens when we die. A common belief amongst Christian groups is: if we are good, we go to Heaven, but if we are evil, we go to Hell. But what does the Bible actually say?

1. Remember **Romans 3:12 (ESV)** where it says, "No one does good, not even one". Being good does not get you into Heaven or make you "right" with God.

2. The only way to salvation is through Jesus Christ. In **Romans 10:13 (ESV)**, "everyone who calls on the name of the Lord **will be saved**"!

Even though everyone who calls on Jesus will be saved, this does not tell us what happens when we die. It only tells us who **will be saved**. It doesn't matter whether we do good or evil as long as we call on the name of the Lord, we will be saved...period. Besides, being saved **DOES NOT** mean we go to Heaven when we die.

3. Once you are dead, you are gone. Your brain doesn't function. You know nothing. You are dead!

4. And, whether you are good or evil, you both end up the same way...dead, face up, six feet under. Both the righteous and the wicked share the same destiny.

Read it for yourself, right there in the Bible. This is an eye opener that no one wants to talk about.

Ecclesiastes 9:1-6 (ESV)

> v1 But, all this I laid to heart, examining it all, how the righteous and the wise and their deeds are in the hand of God. Whether it is love or hate, man does not know; both are before Him. v2 It is the same for all, since **the same event happens to the righteous and the wicked, to the good and the evil**, to the clean and the unclean, to him who sacrifices and him who does not sacrifice.

As the good one is, so is the sinner, and he who swears is as he who shuns an oath. v3 This is an evil in all that is done under the sun, that **the same event happens to all**. Also, the hearts of the children of man are full of evil, and madness is in their hearts while they live, and after that they go to the dead. v4 But, he who is joined with all the living has hope, for a living dog is better than a dead lion. v5 For, the living know that they will die, but **the dead know nothing, and they have no more reward,** for the memory of them is forgotten. v6 Their love and their hate and their envy have already perished, and **forever** they have no more share, in all that is done, under the sun.

And, if we go back to **Ecclesiastes 3:19-20 (ESV)**, where it says "For what happens to the children of man and what happens to the beasts is the same; **as one dies, so dies the other**. They all have the same breath, and man has no advantage over the beasts, for all is vanity". v20 "**All go to one place. All are from the dust, and to dust all return**".

5. Is David, a man after God's own heart, in Heaven?

6. No, because no man has gone to Heaven!

According to **Acts 2:29 (ESV)**, David, a man after God's own heart, the King of Israel, and the ancestor of Jesus, died and was buried and his tomb was still with us many years after he died. So, even David did not go to Heaven.

Acts 2:29 (ESV) says, "Brothers, I may say to you **with confidence** about the patriarch David that he both **died and was buried**, and his tomb is with us to this day".

Then, it clearly says in **John 3:13 (ESV)**, "**And no man hath ascended into heaven, but He that descended out of heaven, even the Son of man, which is in heaven**".

Remember earlier, we saw that sometimes a clear statement in the Bible may appear to contradict other statements in the Bible. When that happens, the clear statement is always right. This statement is about as clear as any statement in the Bible... **No Man Has Ascended into Heaven**. Period! Then what did Jesus mean when He said to the thief on the cross in **Luke 23:43 (ESV)** today He would be with him in paradise?

Keep in mind that the original text did not use punctuation. So, when the English version says "Truly, I say to you, today you will be with me in paradise." Is Jesus saying literally that He would see him that same day? Is He saying, "I'll meet you up there in a little while", "Later Bro", "I'll see you this afternoon"? NO! Because that would contradict the very clear statement that **No Man Has Ascended into Heaven**.

So, what was Jesus saying? Well, without the punctuation, Jesus is saying "I say to you today" or "Today I say to you" or "As of Today I say". In other words, today is the day that He's telling him that he is guaranteed to be with Him in paradise, but it's not the actual day he's leaving to go to paradise.

I know this is a shocker, but the Bible clearly says that **No man has gone to Heaven**. This is **NOT** Randy's ideas or interpretation. This is straight up from the Bible. Then, why so much hype about going to Heaven when we die. The Bible clearly says **No Man Has Ascended into Heaven**. There is so much urban myth out there that people tend to believe the urban myth more than they believe God.

WHAT IS AN IMMORTAL SOUL?

I know all of this is shocking and most of these things are contrary to what you've heard or what you've been taught, but here is another shocker, so hold on to your seat. This one definitely goes against everything you have been taught. So here it goes...**there is NO such thing as an Immortal Soul**. Why would I even say that? Why would I risk my entire reputation on such a bold statement? Simply, because it **DOES NOT** exist. It cannot be found anywhere in the Bible. The idea of an Immortal Soul is nothing more than Urban Myth.

Take a look at **I Timothy 6:15-16 (ESV)**, where Paul is writing to Timothy in v15, referring to Jesus, "He will display at the proper time—He who is the blessed and only Sovereign, the King of kings and Lord of lords", v16 "**who alone has immortality**, who dwells in unapproachable light, whom no one has ever seen or can see. To him be honor and eternal dominion. Amen".

Here we have Jesus, Lord of lords, King of kings, the only one who has immortality. We **DO NOT** have immortality or an immortal soul. If we had an immortal soul, that would make our soul immortal, but the Bible clearly says, Jesus alone has immortality.

Some religious beliefs are based on false assumptions. And, when you have false assumption, you end up with a false conclusion. One of these false assumptions is that we have an Immortal Soul that continues to live on after our physical bodies die, whether in Heaven or in Hell. However, that is simply **NOT TRUE,** it is **NOT** in the Bible. It's nothing more than an **urban myth.** Once again, this is **NOT** Randy's idea. This is straight up from the Bible.

However, the word soul is in some translations of the Bible, but it is **NOT** immortal. It eats when we eat, it lives when we live, and it dies when we die. In fact, the word soul was translated from a Hebrew word that means creature. We do not have an immortal soul, we **ARE** a soul, a creature. In effect, a human creature that dies like all other creatures. The same Hebrew word in the Bible is used for both soul and creature.

In **Genesis 1:21 (ESV)**, it says "God created the great sea **creatures** and every living **creature** that moves, with which the waters swarm, according to their kinds, and every winged bird according to its kind".

And in **Genesis 1:24 (ESV)**, it says "Let the earth bring forth living **creatures** according to their kinds—livestock and creeping things and beasts of the earth according to their kinds".

Then in **Genesis 2:7 (ESV)**, it says "then the Lord God formed the man of dust from the ground and breathed into his nostrils the breath of life, and the man became a living **creature**".

Basically, the same Hebrew word used for great sea creatures in **Genesis 1:21 (ESV)** and living **creatures** and beasts in **Genesis 1:24 (ESV)** is the same Hebrew word used to describe Human **creatures**, sometimes translated as the word "Soul" or "Living Soul", but **NEVER** Immortal Soul.

Then God says to Adam, a living soul / creature, in **Genesis 3:19 (ESV)**, "By the sweat of your face you shall eat bread, till you return to the ground, for out of it you were taken; for you are dust, and to dust you shall return". Adam is dust and so are we, a living soul, a living creature. **NOT** an Immortal Soul. The answer to the question, what happens when we die, is right there in **Genesis 3:19 (ESV), we will return to the ground and to dust we shall return.**

As you can see from the scriptures above, the Bible clearly says, once you are dead you are dead.

1. David is in the Tomb...still dead.

2. Heaven exists, but **NO** man has ascended to Heaven.

3. There is **NO** such thing as an Immortal Soul.

4. We are dust and to dust we shall return.

5. When we die, we are dead, in the grave, six feet under.

6. We **DO NOT** go to Heaven.

But Wait! That is still not the end of the story.

So, back to **Genesis 2:7 (ESV)**, where it says, "then the Lord God formed the man of dust from the ground and breathed into his nostrils the breath of life, and the man became a **living creature**". Here we see that God breathed into us the breath of life. This breath of God is what is referred to as **The Spirit in Man.**

This essence, this spirit in man, is what gives us life, makes us understand and gives us intelligence as explained in **Job 32:8 (ESV)**, where it says, "But it is the spirit in man, the breath of the Almighty, that **makes him understand**". Then it says it again in **Job 33:4 (ESV)**, "The Spirit of God has made me, and the breath of the Almighty **gives me life**". Not only does the breath of God, **which is the spirit in man**, make us understand, but it also gives us life. Without it, we would be nothing more than an "action figure".

The Bible does not talk much about the spirit in man, maybe just a few scriptures here and there, mostly in Job. Although, it is clear, that the sprit in man is what gives us physical life. However, it is **NOT** an immortal soul. Nowhere in the Bible can you find evidence of an immortal soul. As you can see from some of the scriptures in **Ecclesiastes**, we saw earlier, that both the righteous and the wicked die the same death and return to the dust of the ground. And just like man dies so does the beast. We all die the same death and return to the dust of the ground.

Then, in **Ecclesiastes 12:1-7 (ESV)**, the overall theme here is remembering the creator in your youth. In v1, it says "Remember also your Creator in the days of your youth, before the evil days come and the years draw near of which you will say, I have no pleasure in them". Throughout v2-7, it is saying the same thing in different ways. Remember the creator while you still can, before the sun fades, before the door shuts, etc. Basically, remember the creator before you die and then it gets to v7, it is saying remember the creator before, "the dust returns to the earth as it was, and the spirit returns to God who gave it". This is the only place in the Bible that says what happens to the Sprit in Man when you die. The theme or subject of this group of scriptures is not about the Spirit in Man, it just referenced it.

We already know we will all die the same death and we **DO NOT** go to Heaven, but instead return to the dust of the ground. However, the spirit in man, whether we are good or evil, that same spirit that gave us life, returns to God who gave it. It's **NOT US** going to Heaven, it is not an immortal soul. It is God's breath, which gave us understanding, the spirit God **loaned** us so we could have physical life. Once we are dead, we don't need it anymore, so it goes back to God who gave it. Then what does God do with it once He gets it back? I have no idea. Maybe, since the Spirit in Man is the breath of God, a little piece of God that he loaned us, He just takes it back. Or, perhaps He holds onto it for now and then gives it back to us once He resurrects the dead. Either way, it is **NOT** an immortal soul, and it is **NOT** the Holy Spirit. The Holy Spirit is entirely something else, which is a completely different subject on its own.

Now we've discovered that we **DO NOT** go to Heaven and in fact no man has ever gone to Heaven, except for Jesus. Even David, a man after God's own heart, did not go to Heaven. If David did not go, then certainly Abraham, Isaac, and Jacob did not go and neither did Moses or Noah. Although Heaven does exist, there is all this Urban Myth about going to Heaven when we die, but that is just a myth.

So, is that it? We just live this physical life, and we're done...Sayonara, adios, goodbye, see ya. **NO!** There is still more to the story, death is just a resting place, so stay tuned!

WHAT ABOUT HELL?

So, what about Hell? We've talked about Heaven and usually Heaven and Hell come as a package. The most common Christian belief is that when we die, we will go to one place or the other. However, we've read that no one has gone to Heaven when they died. So, what about Hell? Do those who are too far gone go to Hell? Well, we also saw that there is no such thing as an Immortal Soul. In order to go to Hell for an eternity, we would have to be immortal or at least have an immortal soul. Whereas, the Bible clearly said that Jesus is the only one who has immortality. We also saw that both the good and the evil die the same death and return to dust. So, who is going to Hell? Is God **NOT** strong enough, **NOT** powerful enough to reach everyone or rehabilitate them? We've also established that Jesus paid the price for everyone, so no one will be required to pay the price. Besides, Jesus destroyed sin and the works of the devil, including death and Hell.

So, who's going to Hell? Let's take a closer look and see what the Bible actually says about Hell and who's going there. As I mentioned early on, Hell is one of those old English words that are not used in modern English, unless it is in connection with the Bible or used as an exclamatory expression.

If you do some research on the Old English definition of the word Hell, it simply means to cover or conceal. Back in the day and I mean way back in the day around the early 1600's, the term Hell was used by potato farmers. It was a common practice for potato farmers to put their potatoes in "Hell" to preserve them. This was to keep the potatoes from sprouting eyes. Basically, they would take the harvested potatoes and put them in a pit or a box and then cover them to keep the sunlight out. This would minimize spoilage and keep the potatoes from sprouting eyes, which are poisonous.

Let's take a look at what the Old Testament says about Hell. First, let's take a look at **Genesis 37**. Here we find the story of Joseph and his brothers, the sons of Jacob. Remember they are from the line of Abraham. It was Abraham, Isaac, and then Jacob (whose name got changed later to Israel). God had told Abraham He would make him a great nation. Abraham had 12 great grandsons, sons of Jacob.

Commonly known later as the 12 tribes of Israel. Joseph was Jacob's favorite. Some of his brothers were jealous and they hated him, so they plotted to kill him.

Wow! Some great nation, right? Of course, God can work with anyone regardless of who they are. However, instead of killing him, they came across an opportunity to sell their brother into slavery instead. Then, they lied to their father and told him that Joseph was attacked and killed by a wild animal.

Once their father Jacob believed Joseph was dead, we read in **Genesis 37:34-35 (ESV)** where it says in v34 "Then Jacob tore his garments and put sackcloth on his loins and mourned for his son many days." v35 "All his sons and all his daughters rose up to comfort him, but he refused to be comforted and said, 'No, I shall go down to Sheol to my son, mourning.'" Whaaat! What kind of word is "Sheol"? That's not even an English word, but it's in the **E**nglish **S**tandard **V**ersion (**ESV**). Well, with a little research, I found out it's a Hebrew word that means "abode of the dead", but there is no easy translation to English, so it was left in the **ESV** as a Hebrew word. Basically, it's where all the dead go to return to dust. In other words, the grave. In fact, the **N**ew **I**nternational **V**ersion (**NIV**) translates v35 "All his sons and daughters came to comfort him, but he refused to be comforted. 'No', he said, 'I will continue to mourn until I join my son in the **grave**'". Upon further investigation, the word abode, which is also an Old English word, means a **waiting place**. In other words, the dead are in the grave waiting. **Waiting for what?** We will look into that a little later.

Notice something very interesting. Jacob understood that if Joseph was dead, he went to the grave and then when Jacob dies, he believed that he would join his son in the grave as well. There was no mention of Heaven or Hell, just the grave. And, if you look back at Adam, Cain, and all the wickedness of man at the time of the flood, there was no mention of Heaven or Hell either. Maybe Hell didn't exist yet? Or maybe they all go to the grave and return to dust just like the Bible says.

So, what else is interesting is that nowhere in the **E**nglish **S**tandard **V**ersion **(ESV)** can we find Hell mentioned in the Old Testament. Like I said, maybe it doesn't exist yet. However, we see the word Sheol quite a bit, the abode of the dead, where both the good and evil go when they die. So, in order to do a thorough research, I took a look at the **N**ew **I**nternational **V**ersion **(NIV)**, where we cannot find Hell mentioned in the Old Testament either… interesting. Then I also looked at the **A**merican **S**tandard **V**ersion **(ASV)** and guess what? No mention of Hell in the Old Testament either…very interesting.

So, where does the idea of Hell come from? This fiery pit where sinners go when they die. It does not seem to be in the Old Testament at all. Besides, we've established that we **DO NOT** have an immortal soul, we will all die the same death, both the good and the evil. We've also seen that Jacob's understanding was that he would go to Sheol / the grave and throughout Psalms you can see that David also shared that same belief. None of the religious beliefs of the Old Testament included an alternate destination that involves an eternity of torment in a fiery pit. I'm still thinking maybe Hell doesn't exist yet.

Since Hell is such a big deal then why isn't it mentioned at all in the Old Testament? And what about all the evil people between Adam and Jesus? Where did they go? As we saw earlier, both the righteous and the wicked die the same death and go to the grave to return to dust.

If you think about it, Satan is supposed to be running things down there, but before he was Satan, he was the highly esteemed Lucifer. Although Heaven has always existed as long as God has existed, but Hell could not have existed prior to Lucifer rebelling against God. However, Lucifer rebelled long before man was created, but there was still no mention of Hell in the Old Testament.

Then, once Lucifer rebelled, we see in **Revelation 12:7-14 (ESV)** where it says, "Now war arose in heaven, Michael and his angels fighting against the dragon. And the dragon and his angels fought back, v8 but he was defeated, and there was no longer any place for them in heaven. v9 And, the great dragon was thrown down, that ancient serpent, who is called the devil and Satan, the deceiver of the whole world—he was thrown down to the earth, and his angels were thrown down with him. v10 And I heard a loud voice in heaven, saying, 'Now the salvation and the power and the kingdom of our God and the authority of his Christ have come, for the accuser of our brothers has been thrown down, who accuses them day and night before our God'. v11 And, they have conquered him by the blood of the Lamb and by the word of their testimony, for they loved not their lives even unto death. v12 Therefore, rejoice, O heavens and you who dwell in them! But woe to you, O earth and sea, for the devil has come down to you in great wrath, because he knows that his time is short! v13 And, when the dragon saw that he had been thrown down to the earth, he pursued the woman who had given birth to the male child".

Several things we notice from these scriptures:

1. In v11, they conquered him by the blood of the Lamb, so this must be sometime after Jesus was crucified. It could have been after He ascended to Heaven, or it was possibly during the 40 days after Jesus was resurrected but before He ascended. We are not exactly sure, but it had to be at least sometime after He was crucified.

2. In v9, it refers to Satan as "that ancient serpent". So, by the time Satan was thrown out of Heaven, he was already considered ancient.

3. We also see in v9 and v13 that Satan was thrown down to **earth**. He was **NOT** thrown down to Hell or some fiery pit.

WHAT ABOUT HELL?

4. Prior to Satan being thrown down, he was already Satan, the accuser of the brothers, right there in Heaven, not from Hell. In v10, the authority of Christ was demonstrated by throwing Satan out of Heaven.

5. We also saw earlier in Job, that Satan was in Heaven congregating with God and the other angels. And, when God asked what he as up to, he said "going to and fro on the earth, and from walking up and down on it." He never mentioned anything about hanging out in Hell.

6. We also notice, prior to getting his ass kicked, he was constantly going back and forth between Heaven and earth as we saw in Job, but we also saw Satan, aka the serpent, alive and well back in the Garden. But we never saw him in Hell.

7. As you can see from v4-6 above that Satan has been in Heaven all that time, not Hell, until Christ took over, then he was thrown down to **earth**, not Hell.

8. Then, once Satan was thrown down, we notice in v12, that he knows his time is short.

9. If Satan's time is short, how can anyone go to Hell for an eternity...Satan's days are already numbered.

10. And we also read earlier that Jesus destroyed the works of the devil, including sin, death, and Hell.

Now, let's go back to the Old Testament for a minute. We see during the 1600 years between Adam and Noah, there is nothing mentioned about anyone going to Hell. Then if we fast forward between Noah and Jesus, we still don't see anyone going to Hell. And the Hebrew word Sheol is sometimes translated as pit or grave, which tells me that pit and grave are the same thing as the abode of the dead.

Even though, some English translations of the Bible, including the King James version, does use the word Hell, it **DOES NOT** refer to some fiery pit where sinners go. Besides, the definition of Hell is to cover or conceal, so how does that have anything to do with a fiery pit that torments forever? **It doesn't!**

The Hebrew word Sheol, the abode of the dead, has been translated as pit, grave, and sometimes Hell (cover or conceal). This makes sense that Sheol, the abode of the dead, would be the grave or pit where we bury the dead and then what do we do, we close a casket or **cover** the grave with dirt, in effect putting the body into Hell just like the potato farmer puts the potatoes into Hell.

I know this is in complete contradiction to what you've been taught, but it's all right there in your Bible. The idea of a fiery pit of torment called "Hell" is so popular that most people will dismiss the simple truth found in the Bible and believe the Urban Myth instead. Even if you went to Seminary (Bible College) and you studied these scriptures and you **are sure** you know what they mean, I'm asking you to re-study these scriptures and take another look. Even if some of the scriptures in the Old Testament sound like they could be talking about some kind of furnace or they might imply something similar to **YOUR** idea of Hell, in a vague kind of way, you really have to stretch your imagination to read into it that way. And because of this pre-conceived, wide-spread idea about "Hell", a lot of people read into these scriptures things that are **NOT** there.

Now we've seen some real scriptures of what the Bible actually says, in black and white. Everything else is Urban Myth. Besides, the word Hell doesn't even have anything to do with a fiery pit of torment. It's just an Old English word that means to cover or conceal. The translators sometimes use this word to describe the abode of the dead (waiting place). And other times they translated it pit or grave. And, as we saw earlier, several versions of the English Bible don't even use the word Hell at all in their Old Testament translations.

But wait a minute! That's the Old Testament. Maybe Hell doesn't exist yet. What about the New Testament?

First of all, none of this is adding up.

1. We've read that Jesus paid the price for everyone, but many still believe that sinners go to Hell. If Jesus paid the price for everyone, then the price is already paid. So, who is going to Hell?

2. We've also read that all have Sinned and fall short of the glory of God.

3. If all have sinned and sinners go to Hell, then **ALL** of us go to Hell.

4. We've also read that the Wages of Sin is Death, but the gift of God is eternal life.

5. But many believe that sinners spend eternal life in Hell. That would make Hell a gift of God as well... Yay! Thanks God.

6. Besides, death is death. If God means Hell, then why didn't He just say that? Or is He lying?

None of this is adding up. Let's explore the New Testament to see what the Bible actually says.

We can see from the scriptures above that Hell DID NOT exist in the Old Testament as a fiery pit where sinners go to be tortured and tormented for an eternity. However, if it did exist, it would have been a big deal. So why didn't God mention it before and why didn't anyone talk about it. It was not even part of their culture or religious beliefs at the time. Besides, Satan was still in Heaven roaming back and forth from Heaven and earth, as we saw earlier.

However, once we get to the New Testament, Jesus certainly seemed to be talking about it. Why now? Why all of a sudden did Jesus start bringing it up? Did God just now create Hell once Jesus came around?

If God just created Hell, then why didn't He say that? But instead, Jesus starts talking about it like everyone should know what He's talking about. He acts like it's been there forever. But we saw earlier that it never came up before in the Old Testament and it wasn't part of their culture or religious beliefs. So why isn't anyone asking Jesus, "dude, what are you talking about?" Instead, everyone is just chillin'. Things just aren't adding up. Let's see what Jesus actually says about it.

Now, the first time Hell is ever mentioned in the entire Bible, English Standard Version **(ESV),** is in **Matthew 5:22 (ESV)**. Let's start in v21 for context where Jesus says, "You have heard that it was said to those of old, 'You shall not murder; and whoever murders will be liable to judgment". Here Jesus is quoting one of the Old Testament laws and His purpose is to expound upon the law. Then we go to v22 where He says," But I say to you that everyone who is angry with his brother will be liable to judgment; whoever insults (translated from a Greek word that means abuses) his brother will be liable to the council; and whoever says, 'You fool!' will be liable to the Hell of fire".

Wow! There it is...Hell fire or Hell of fire. If you call someone a fool, you go to Hell. Geeze! That is harsh. If you murder or you're angry, you are only liable to judgement, if you abuse your brother, you face the consequences of the council. But if you and your buddy are hanging out, shooting pool and you're just messing around and you call him a fool, you go to Hell. That doesn't even make sense. Seems like murder would get you a ticket to Hell, but instead it's calling someone a fool.

Besides, it seems odd that the first time Hell is mentioned in the Bible is when Jesus just casually throws it out there in a conversation where He is expounding upon the law. He never explained what He meant by Hell of fire. And what is even more strange is that nobody asked him what he was talking about. Seems like someone would have at least said "what are you talking about bro". Maybe they understood what He was saying. But how did they know? It wasn't part of the religious beliefs of the day. Something is still not adding up.

If you recall, the word Hell is an Old English word that means to cover or conceal. However, the translators would sometimes use the word Hell to describe a pit or a grave. In this case, since the New Testament was written in Greek, the translators used the Old English word Hell to translate the Greek word Gehenna, which refers to the Hebrew place called Ge-Hinnom (The Valley of Hinnom). In Greek it is Gehenna, which is a physical valley located just outside the walls of Jerusalem. It was a giant **pit** (translated hell) used as a kind of dumping ground, like a city dump (garbage dump).

They would keep the fire going like a furnace to burn up all the refuse. People would throw their animal carcasses there amongst other things into the pit. Prior to it being a general dumping ground, it was used by the ancient Kings of Judah as a place for child sacrifices. It must have had a really bad reputation.

So, when Jesus used the expression Hell of fire as in **Matthew 5:22 (ESV)** and some other scriptures we will look at, he is basically saying **Pit of Fire**, which is Gehenna. This may be where the idea, the Urban Myth came from about a fiery pit of torment called Hell. When actually it was just a dumping ground called Gehenna that the translators used the Old English word Hell to describe it.

Everyone in the area of Jerusalem knew about the Valley of Hinnom, this fiery pit used as a garbage dump. However, when the translators used the Old English word Hell to describe it, Jesus was not talking about a fiery pit where sinners go to be tortured and tormented for eternity. Now it makes sense why no one questioned Him about it.

It was common for Jesus to make up stories and use parables to get His point across. A lot of what He said was not meant literally, but for the purpose of getting a spiritual principle across to his followers and anyone else within listening range. Even the expression "Born Again" was not meant literally. However, Nicodemus took Him literally and he asked Jesus for clarification. We see throughout Jesus' journey; His disciples and other followers will ask questions for clarification if they don't understand something. Although, no one seemed to ask Him about the Hell of fire. Why? Because it was common knowledge. They knew He was talking about the garbage dump.

Then we see In **Matthew 5:29-30 (ESV)**, where Jesus says in v29 "If your right eye causes you to sin, tear it out and throw it away. For it is better that you lose one of your members than that your whole body be thrown into Hell. v30 And, if your right hand causes you to sin, cut it off and throw it away. For it is better that you lose one of your members than that your whole body go into Hell".

Once again, Jesus is talking about Gehenna. This Valley of refuge. He is not talking about literally cutting your hand off or plucking out your eye. He is trying to illustrate His point. They knew what He meant. They didn't even question Him about it. He was **NOT** talking about going to a Hell fire and torment for an eternity.

Just because the word Hell generates images in your head of a fiery pit of torment, doesn't mean that's what the Bible actually says. As you can see, it is an Old English word that the translators used to describe a pit, a grave, or garbage dump. Jesus **NEVER** mentions a fiery pit where sinners go to be tormented and neither does the rest of the Bible.

In **Matthew 10 (ESV)**, Jesus is talking to his Apostles and giving them a pep talk as He sends them out to proclaim the Gospel. Then we get to v28, where He says

"And do not fear those who kill the body but cannot kill the soul. Rather fear him who can destroy both soul and body in hell". Basically, man can kill the body, but God can destroy the body and soul in Hell.

We will look at some more scriptures in a little bit, but several things jump out immediately in v28.

1. Here we see the expression body and soul. We saw in the Old Testament that the translators used the Old English word **soul** sometimes to describe a creature. However, in the New Testament the Old English word **soul** was also used, but this time it was translated from the Greek word "psyche". When we see the word psyche, we think of our mind. That is basically what Jesus is saying when He says body and soul (body and mind).

2. However, the translators used the word soul to describe "psyche". They also translated "psyche" into other English expressions or words such as "to myself" (to my soul), "I" (my soul), "their minds" (their souls), "of us" (souls), "human beings" (human souls).

3. As you can see, the word soul was an Old English word that the translators used to describe various attributes of the human creature. However, the word soul was **NEVER** used to describe an Immortal

Soul or an Immortal Creature. Besides we've already established that there is no such thing as an Immortal Soul.

4. We also see that the body and soul can be **DESTROYED**. This is **NOT** some kind of eternal existence where we get tortured and tormented in a fiery pit forever.

5. Besides, Jesus was just referencing Gehenna in order to illustrate his point, which is to fear God rather than man.

In **Matthew 16:18 (ESV)**, Jesus says "And I tell you, you are Peter, and on this rock I will build my church, and the gates of Hell shall not prevail against it". In this case, the translators used the Old English word Hell to describe the Greek word "Hades", which means the underground abode of the dead. In other words, the grave. Once again, Jesus was NOT referring to a fiery pit of torment and torture.

Then in **Matthew 18:9 (ESV)**, it says "And if your eye causes you to sin, tear it out and throw it away. It is better for you to enter life with one eye than with two eyes to be thrown into the Hell of fire". Basically, Jesus is saying the same thing He said back in **Matthew 5:29-30 (ESV)**. The Hell of fire, Hell fire, or fiery pit is the same word used for Gehenna. It's a specific spot outside of

Jerusalem and not a fiery pit where sinners go to get tortured and tormented.

This is interesting! Jesus is talking symbolically, using the expressions of the day as an analogy. He keeps referencing Gehenna (the garbage dump). Now, let me clarify something for a minute. Jesus was **NOT** being literal, so don't go and pluck out your eye. Based on other clear scriptures, Jesus is the only way to get rid of sin.

In **Matthew 23 (ESV)**, Jesus is talking to the Scribes and the Pharisees. He is calling them out and tells them they're all a bunch of Hypocrites. We see that in v15, He says "Woe to you, scribes and Pharisees, hypocrites! For you travel across sea and land to make a single proselyte, and when he becomes a proselyte, you make him twice as much a child of Hell as yourselves. A proselyte is another Old English word that means a person that converts from one religion to another, such as Christian to Judaism. Then continuing down to v33, we see another reference to Hell, where He says, "You serpents, you brood of vipers, how are you to escape being sentenced to Hell?" Wow! Jesus is fired up and letting them "have it".

The expression Jesus used when He said to the Pharisees that they make the proselyte twice as much a child of Hell (garbage dump) as themselves is like calling them a piece of trash, since Hell was nothing more than a trash heap called Gehenna. Then when He calls them serpents and brood of vipers, He was not suggesting that anyone was going to "Hell". Some translations say damnation to Hell in v33, but either way it was a rhetorical question and not meant literally. It's like saying "With that attitude, how do you plan on escaping a life of trouble (life full of garbage)" or "sentenced to a troubled life full of garbage".

We know from the previous examples that Jesus talks in parables and makes up stories. He uses common expressions of the day as well as analogies. A lot of what he says is just to get His point across and not meant literally, which takes us to **Matthew 25**.

In **Matthew 25:14-30 (ESV)**, we see the story (parable) of the talents. A man went away and while he was gone, he gave one of his servants five talents for safe keeping, another servant he entrusted with two, and a third one was only given one talent. When the man returned, the servant that was given just one talent hid it away and did not make a profit. Then in v29-30, it says v29 "For to everyone who has, will more be given, and he will have an abundance. But from the one who has not, even what he has, will be taken away". v30 "And cast the worthless servant into the **outer darkness**. In that place there will be weeping and gnashing of teeth".

This story tells about the worthless servant being cast into **outer darkness**. This is an expression, and it **DOES NOT** say or even imply that this **outer darkness** is Hell. Sure, you can read into it that way but that's just imagination. All it says is cast into **outer darkness**. In that place of **outer darkness**, it says, there will be weeping and gnashing of teeth. Again, it **DOES NOT** say that place is Hell. We can assume it's Hell, but if the Bible doesn't clearly say that, then it's only an assumption. First of all, Jesus made up this story and He's talking in parables, so it is reasonable that this **outer darkness** is just an expression and not meant literally. If there is no Hell, then He can't be talking about Hell anyway. If there is a Hell, then why didn't He just say that. These scriptures are talking in parables, and they give a very vague description. Besides, weeping and gnashing of teeth was a common expression that meant sorrow and regret. Just like the expression tongue and cheek, means sarcastic or humorous. These are just expressions.

Basically, that's all Jesus had to say about Hell. First, we see that Hell was never mentioned in the Old Testament. Then, when Jesus talked about it, He was referring to the pit of fire called Gehenna that was used as a garbage dump. Jesus **NEVER** mentioned, **NOT EVEN ONCE,** a fiery pit where sinners go to be tormented and tortured.

If you notice, the books of Matthew, Mark, Luke, and John are similar accounts of the same events and the same conversations. These guys would follow Jesus around and write down their observations of what they saw and the conversations they heard at the time. So, when Jesus mentioned the garbage dump, He only mentioned it seven times in the entire Bible...ONLY seven times. All seven accounts were recorded right there in Matthew. Then the translators used the Old English word Hell to describe the garbage dump. Mark recorded three of those conversations and Luke only recorded it once. Then, when we take a look at John's account of the events, he never mentions it.

For now, let's recap some of the things we've discovered.

1. God made Adam with human nature and gave him free choice, which is a deadly combination for making bad choices.

2. God knew that before Adam was even created. It was all part of God's original plan and design from the beginning.

3. That's why Jesus was slain from the foundation of the world. It was part of the plan.

4. God does not punish humans for acting like humans. That's how He designed us…to act like humans.

5. We have free choice about our behavior as long as we stay within the framework of God's plan. We do not get a choice about anything that is contrary to God's plan or falls outside the framework of God's plan.

6. And our free choice does not stop God from fulfilling His free choice and His promise that in Adam **ALL** die, but in Jesus we **ALL** live.

7. We have all sinned and fall short of the glory of God, but Jesus paid the price for everyone.

8. We found out that when we die, we return to dust and that no one has gone to Heaven, but there's still more to the story.

9. We also discovered that likewise, no one goes to Hell. The Hell that people imagine, doesn't exist. It's just an Urban Myth and **NOT** in the Bible.

A commonly misunderstood scripture is **Matthew 25:41 (ESV)**, but for context let's start in v31, where it says "When the Son of Man **comes in his glory**, and all the angels with him, then he will sit on his glorious throne. v32 Before him will be gathered all the nations, and he will **separate people** one from another as a shepherd separates the sheep from the goats. v33 And, he will place the sheep on his right, but the goats on the left. v34 Then the King will say to those on his right, 'Come, you who are blessed by my Father, inherit the kingdom prepared for you from the foundation of the world".

Then the thought continues in v41, where it says, "Then he will say to those on his left, 'Depart from me, you cursed, into the eternal fire prepared for the devil and his angels".

On the surface, that sounds like the people classified as "goats" are cursed to Hell. However, that is just an assumption. The Bible never says this is Hell.

1. Not only does the Bible **NOT** say this is Hell, but prior to this, it wasn't mentioned in the Old Testament and Jesus **NEVER** talks about an eternal Hell fire where sinners go. So, this must be referring to something else.

2. If this **is** some kind of punishment, then punishment for what? Jesus already paid the price for **ALL** sin.

3. Not to mention, we read in **Hebrews 9:28 (ESV)** that when Jesus returns the second time He is **NOT** dealing with sin.

4. At this point, we have no idea what this eternal fire is, other than we know it was prepared for the devil and his angels. So, we can't just assume it's Hell.

5. However, it does sound like it could be the lake of fire, but then again, the lake of fire can't be Hell either. We will take a look that in Revelation.

6. Although, it is very interesting that the translators used the word Hell to describe the Gehenna garbage dump, but Hell was never used to describe the lake of fire. Why? Because Gehenna and the Lake of Fire are two completely different things.

7. Earlier, we saw God separating everyone into two teams. The believers and the unbelievers. Here we see Jesus separating everyone into two teams, the sheep, and the goats.

8. Besides, we learned earlier that it is God who causes us to be born again and it is God who does all the work. So, who are these "goats" on His left? Remember God does everything in order, according to His plan. For now, the sheep move to the front of the line and the goats have to wait their turn. Just like the team of believers and the team of unbelievers.

9. This sounds like it's the same plan, the same rules John was explaining in John 3:16-18. Not to mention all the other scriptures we've seen that are saying the same thing. This indicates that God is being consistent, and everything is going as planned.

10. Two teams, two groups...everything in order. Two harvests, two resurrections.

In the meantime, notice something interesting. In **Jude (ESV)** we see the **angels** who sinned were in chains. And the burning fire of Sodom and Gomorrah served as an example. Then, here in **Matthew 25:41 (ESV)** we see that the eternal fire was prepared for the devil and his angels. They are not there yet. They are still in chains. And these goats were told to depart into the eternal fire, but it was not prepared for humans. It was prepared for the devil and his angels. Besides, it does not say anything about sinning people going there for the purpose of punishment. In fact, there is **NO** mention of punishment, period! And, the eternal fire of Sodom and Gomorrah, which was the example, eventually burned out, so this eternal fire was not the everlasting, forever kind of fire. **It is temporary**.

Now the most interesting part is in v31 where it says, "When the Son of Man **comes in his glory**", but we read in **Hebrews 9:28 (ESV)** that when Jesus returns the second time He is **NOT** dealing with sin. **So, what is it?** Is Jesus only bringing salvation as it says in **Hebrews 9:28 (ESV)** or is He lying. Since God cannot lie, then the eternal fire prepared for the devil and his angels **CANNOT** be Hell or some kind of punishment for sin, especially since Jesus is not dealing with sin when He **comes in His glory**.

Then, when we get to the section on Revelation, we will see Satan and his angels thrown into the lake of fire. So, it's making sense that this fire prepared for the devil and his angels could be referring to the lake of fire.

Since Jesus never mentioned Hell as a place where sinners go, let's examine the Bible beyond Jesus' words to see if other scriptures are consistent with what Jesus said.

First, I want you to notice Paul for a minute. He was the most prolific writer of the New Testament, an educated man, and a lawyer. He wrote letters to the Romans, Corinthians, Galatians, Ephesians, and many others, but he **NEVER** mentioned Hell, not once...interesting.

A lot of people think the lake of fire is Hell, but it isn't! Jesus never said it was Hell, the translators never used the word Hell to describe it, and the Book of Revelation never calls it Hell. Just because the devil and his angels will be there, doesn't mean it's Hell. And, if it was the same thing that Jesus was talking about when he referenced the garbage dump, then why didn't the translators use the word Hell to describe it? What does the Bible actually say? We will look into that as it relates to the lake of fire in the section about Revelation.

When reading earlier that every knee will bow and every tongue will confess, and that Jesus came to destroy the works of the devil, it's making more sense why Jesus never mentioned Hell. Since every tongue will confess, then there will be no need for Hell.

But then we get to **II Peter 2:4-9 (ESV)**, Peter was illustrating God's abilities by giving some examples. He said if God did not spare the angels that sinned in v2 and if He did not spare the ancient world, except for Noah in v3 and so on, then in v9 Peter's point is: if God did all that, then He certainly knows how to rescue the Godly from trials.

However, in the midst of Peter's encouraging words, he says in v4 "For if God did not spare angels when they sinned but cast them into Hell and committed them to chains of gloomy darkness to be kept until the judgment". Wow! Now that's sounding more like the Hell we've heard so much about.

Let's think about this for a minute...

1. Peter was just using this reference as one of his examples to make his point.

2. Peter was NOT trying to define or expound on the properties of Hell.

3. Hell was never mentioned in the Old Testament.

4. Hell was never mentioned by Jesus.

5. Hell was never brought up by Paul, James, or the other apostles.

6. So why, all of a sudden, would Peter bring it up now?

7. And, if Hell is such a big deal, then why is it only mentioned this one time?

8. None of this is adding up.

9. Peter must have been talking about something else and not the Hell we imagine it to be.

So, what was Peter talking about? In this case, the Greek word used was Tartarus, which the translators used the Old English word Hell to translate into English. So, what is Tartarus? Tartarus means a place of restraint. Now that makes sense, since God cast the angels who sinned to a place of restraint and as Peter said, committed them to chains of gloomy darkness. It was only used this one time. Only once in the entire Bible and only in reference to angels that sinned and NOT humans.

It was also used In Greek mythology where Tartarus was considered the lowest Hell beyond Hades where the Titans were sent and restrained once they were defeated by Zeus. But then again, that is just mythology.

Peter is pointing out that Satan and his demons have been defeated by God. And according to **Revelation 12 (ESV)**, as we read earlier, they were cast down from Heaven to **earth**. In effect, earth would be a place of restraint, a prison, for them, not some fiery pit called Hell.

Once again, we see all these scriptures using the Old English word Hell, but none of them refer to a fiery pit where sinners go when they die. There seems to be a clear dis-connect between the common concept of Hell as a place of torment and torture for eternity and what the Bible actually says.

Even though we don't see Hell mentioned in Paul's writings and we don't see Jesus mentioning it either, except when he references the garbage dump, let's see what He says about Lazarus and the rich man in **Luke 16 (ESV)**. It starts out with Jesus telling the parable about a rich man and his accountant who embezzled money from him. Jesus made up this story to get the point across that you can't serve two masters. You can't serve God and money. Then Jesus continues in v14-16, where he's talking about the Pharisees, who love money and they were holding on to the law and the prophets when they should be following the good news of the Kingdom of God instead. Then in v18, Jesus is talking about divorce and remarriage. That seems random, but I guess Jesus was on a roll that day.

Now we get to Lazarus and the Rich Man. The last in a series of made-up stories by Jesus in **Luke 16, v19-31 (ESV)**. In v22, they both die, according to Jesus' story, where it says "The poor man died and was carried by the angels to Abraham's side. The rich man also died and was buried". Earlier we saw that no man has ascended to Heaven and that all men return to dust. So, when Jesus was telling His story, He was speaking figuratively and NOT literally. Neither Abraham nor the poor man were in Heaven.

Abraham was the father of the faithful, so the poor man must have died a man of faith. Being carried to Abraham's side is an expression we still use to this day. When a husband and wife are wanting to settle an argument, they may go to their friends. Then, I might say I'm on John's **side** and you might say you're on Suzie's **side**. It's basically the same thing, the poor man was on Abraham's side. In v22, the Bible clearly says that the rich man was buried. He didn't go to Hell; he was simply buried to return to dust.

Then we see in v23, it says "and in Hades, being in torment, he lifted up his eyes and saw Abraham far off and Lazarus at his side". Remember, Hades is Greek word that means the grave or a place of the dead. It's also a continuation from v22 where it said, "The rich man also died and was buried v23 And in Hades".

He was **buried** and in torment in the grave, not in Hell. Then, while dead in the grave, he lifted up his eyes. That is **NOT** even possible! Then again, it's a made-up story. Jesus said he died and was buried. **Notice this**! As Jesus is telling His story, even He knows that when people die, they are buried. There was no mention of Heaven or Hell. Besides, we read earlier that the dead know nothing, so we know this parable is not literal. Then when Jesus uses the word torment, it is an expression that means regret. How many times have you done something in your life that you've regretted, and it torments you the rest of your life? The rich man never became a man of faith, and he died regretting it.

I've heard some say this parable means that the rich man is in Hell. But Hell was never mentioned anywhere else, so why would Jesus suddenly bring it up in the middle of a made-up story in such a mysterious, vague kind of way? Besides if Jesus meant Hell, then why didn't He just say that?

Although, we do have a few scriptures where the Bible talks about Eternal fire, Eternal destruction or Eternal punishment. So, what are they talking about? Well, in **II Thessalonians 1 (ESV)**, Paul, Sylvanus, and Timothy are writing to the Church of the Thessalonians about being thankful to God for the increased faith and love God gave them. And they were boasting about the Church and how strong they have been while enduring persecutions and afflictions.

Then, Paul says in v5-9 that God considers it just to repay those that afflict you with affliction on them. He will inflict vengeance on those that don't know Him, and they will suffer the punishment of **Eternal Destruction**. If Paul doesn't say this is Hell, then we can't just assume that. When we die and go to the grave our bodies are destroyed, and death is an Eternal Destruction until we are resurrected. Not an eternal existence in a fiery pit. Remember, we DO NOT have an immortal soul.

As we read above, Eternal Fire, Eternal Destruction and Eternal punishment DOES NOT mean an Eternal

Existence in a fiery pit. Quite the contrary. The wages of sin is death. Death means death. Death can be an eternity, so that would be an Eternal Punishment of death, or our bodies are destroyed for eternity, which is Eternal Destruction as mentioned before. And, what about Eternal Fire? That's a fire that burns for a long time. Just because the fire burns for a long time or an eternity, doesn't mean we are in it burning up over and over again. **NO WHERE** in the Bible does it mention anything about sinners living an Eternal Life in a fiery pit called Hell, especially since Eternal Life is a free gift from God.

Continuing our thought in **Jude 1:6-7 (ESV)**, God kept the angels who sinned in "**eternal**" chains until the Judgment of the Great Day, just like Sodom and Gomorrah underwent a punishment of "**eternal**" fire as an example. Although, we know it burned to the ground and the fire eventually went out. So, this is just an expression referring to a fire that was burning for a long time. We also see that the "**eternal**" chains were reserved for the angels who sinned not for humans. You can see that the word "**eternal**", as referenced several times in the Bible, does not always mean everlasting. Eternal chains were temporary. It was until the Judgment of the Great Day.

Go ahead and read **Jude 1:6-7 (ESV)**, where it says v6 "And the angels who did not stay within their own position of authority, but left their proper dwelling, he has kept in eternal chains under gloomy darkness **until the judgment** of the great day". v7 "just as Sodom and Gomorrah and the surrounding cities, which likewise indulged in sexual immorality and pursued unnatural desire, serve as an example by undergoing a punishment of eternal fire".

Also, back in **Matthew 18:8 (ESV)**, it says "And if your hand or your foot causes you to sin, cut it off and throw it away. It is better for you to enter life crippled or lame than with two hands or two feet to be thrown into the eternal fire". Once again, this was just an expression. He was talking about the garbage dump Gehenna, which seems to burn eternally, but we know it doesn't exist anymore.

Based on all the scriptures we were able to find about Hell, we **DO NOT** see any indication or evidence of the existence of Hell or a fiery pit where sinners go for an Eternal Life of punishment. In fact, we find everything else, except that, like we don't have an immortal soul and the dead know nothing and we return to dust in the grave. Besides, Eternal Life is a gift of God and Hell is just an Old English word that means to cover or conceal.

Since, we have no evidence of Hell and Jesus paid the price for **ALL** sin, then what happens to the unbeliever? To get a grasp on that, we need to understand what is meant by repentance and what the Bible means when it talks about God's judgment.

REPENTANCE

I'm sure you've heard about repentance or heard the term repent at some point. It's another one of those Old English words that's not used anymore, but it sounds very religious. You've heard expressions like repent and be baptized or repentance from your sins or similar expressions. However, the word "repent" is not a religious term. It is just an Old English word, and it simply means to change your mind or turn around and change direction.

For instance, you can be walking away from God and turn around and walk towards God. That's repentance. Or you can believe that the law leads to salvation, but then realize that Jesus is the only way to salvation, so you change your beliefs. That's also repentance. But get this...if you are walking towards God and then decide to turn your back on God and reject Him, you have also repented. It has nothing to do with being remorseful and it has nothing to do with sin. It simply means to change your mind or turn around and go in a different direction, whether the direction is towards God or away from God.

When you hear the word repent, what do you think? What is the first thing that comes to your mind? A common thought or belief is that we have to feel regret, remorse, or heartfelt sorrow and repent of our sins. However, repentance has nothing to do with all that. When the Bible says to repent, it **DOES NOT** say repent of our sins, beg God's forgiveness, or feel sorry for what you've done. When the word repent is used in the Bible, it means to turn around and go in a different direction. For instance, turning towards God **FOR** the forgiveness of sins. When the Bible says to turn towards God **FOR** the forgiveness of sins, that is the reason to turn towards God. We are **NOT** repenting **OF** our sins; we are repenting (turning around) **FOR** the forgiveness of our sins. In other words, that is why we should repent, **FOR** the forgiveness of sins.

It has nothing to do with feeling remorseful or having regret. Remember Paul, the anti-Christian terrorist? He didn't seem remorseful for killing Christians. He had nothing to be remorseful about, he was doing the right thing. He was doing his job, in accordance with the law at the time. But then God came along and convinced him that it wasn't the best use of his talents, so Paul repented (changed his mind, changed jobs) and switched teams. In fact, God also repented when He changed His mind and destroyed mankind

Repentance

and went a different direction with Noah and his family. Repentance is any change of heart, good or bad, change of belief, or change in direction.

In the big picture, God created us in this human condition. We have human nature, not God nature. Therefore, we have all sinned and fall short of His glory. And the wages of sin is death. And, since we've all sinned, we all have a death sentence hanging over our head. But then God comes along and says repent (change direction) and move toward God and your sins will be forgiven. In effect, God has backed us in a corner, and He doesn't give us much of a choice. Stay where we are with this death sentence hanging over our head or repent (move towards God) and live.

Let's see how the Bible uses the word repent in different situations. Not only did God repent when He destroyed man back in Genesis, but let's also take a look at Mark's account of John the Baptist, where he says in **Mark 1:4 (ESV)** "John appeared, baptizing in the wilderness and proclaiming a **baptism of repentance** for the forgiveness of sins". Notice that this is a baptism of repentance or a baptism of change **FOR** the forgiveness of sins, not repenting of their sins. What are we supposed to change? And who or what are we turning away from?

Now, Luke makes the same observation in **Luke 3:3 (ESV)**, where he says, "And he went into all the region around the Jordan, proclaiming a baptism of repentance

FOR the forgiveness of sins". Again, what are we supposed to change? It doesn't say.

Then we get to **Acts 2:38 (ESV)**, where Peter says, "Repent and be baptized every one of you in the name of Jesus Christ **FOR** the forgiveness of your sins, and you will receive the gift of the Holy Spirit". Here we see that Peter elaborated some on the question of repentance, whereas the word baptize is another Old English word that means immerse. So basically, we are to repent by turning around, changing direction. Then we should be baptized (immersed) in the name of Jesus Christ. But why? What is the value of that, what do we get out of it? Well, it's **FOR** the forgiveness of sins. But why do we need to immerse ourselves in Jesus for the forgiveness of sins, we already have the animal sacrifices?

Well, apparently Jesus is the only one that can get us off of death row by forgiving us of our sins. I mean the law can't forgive us our sins, so, we need to turn towards Jesus if we want to get out of jail and have our freedom. Okay, now I get it, but what are we turning away from? The common belief is that we are turning away from sin, but the Bible **DOES NOT** say that. We have all sinned and fall short of the glory of God, so turning away from sin has no value. We can't undo our sin. It's too late, we all fall short. But then Jesus came and paid the price for all sin. So, turning away from sin is not going to save us. Jesus already took care of sin. So, what are we turning away from?

Well, back in the day before Jesus, God provided a way for the Jews to cover all their sins. So back then, the Jews were required to obey the law. But as you know, it is impossible to perfectly obey the law without messing up. So, God provided the use of animal sacrifices as the method to cover all their sins. The animal sacrifices did not get rid of their sin. It could only cover them temporarily, so they had to keep repeating the process. But now, John the Baptist and then Peter are both saying turn to Jesus **FOR** the forgiveness of sins...no more animal sacrifices. You are now turning towards Jesus **FOR** forgiveness of sins instead of looking to the law and animal sacrifices as a way to cover all your sins. Not only will Jesus cover all your sins, but He will also take away all your sins completely. In other words, Jesus is a permanent solution. So, when John and Peter were saying turn to Jesus **FOR** the forgiveness of sins, what are we turning away from?

We are turning away from the Law. We are no longer required to obey the law. Whaaat! How can that be? We've read earlier that we can't serve two masters. We can't serve Jesus and serve the law at the same time. Either Jesus saves us or the law along with the animal sacrifices is what saves us. In other words, obeying the law is **NOT** a requirement for salvation! Jesus is!

Now, let me be clear! God DID NOT do away with the Law, it's just that the law is no longer a requirement for salvation. And the Bible is very clear that just because we are liberated from the Law, it's NOT done away with and it's NOT an excuse to go out and start killing or stealing or anything else you want to do. This is not anarchy. There are still consequences!

As an example, in **Hebrews 10:1-4 (ESV)**, we see "For since the Law has but a shadow of the good things to come **instead of the true form** of these realities, it can never, by the same sacrifices that are continually offered every year, make perfect those who draw near. v2 Otherwise, would they not have ceased to be offered, since the worshipers, having once been cleansed, would no longer have any consciousness of sins? v3 But, in these sacrifices there is a reminder of sins every year. v4 For, it is impossible for the blood of bulls and goats to take away sins".

Then in v8-10, it says "When he said above, "You have neither desired nor taken pleasure in sacrifices and offerings and burnt offerings and sin offerings" (these are offered according to the Law), v9 then he added, 'Behold, I have come to do your will.' **He does away with the first**, in order to establish the second. v10 And, by that will we have been sanctified through the offering of the body of Jesus Christ once for all".

It looks like Jesus did away with the first, which means the law and the animal sacrifices. Then He established the second, which is the offering of the body of Jesus. So, does that mean God got rid of the law? NO! It means He did away with the requirement to obey the law. In other words, Jesus Himself is the replacement for the law. When we repent and turn towards Jesus, we are turning away from the law, more specifically, the requirement to obey the law as the way to salvation.

We see in **Acts 11:18 (ESV)** it says, "When they heard these things, they fell silent. And they glorified God, saying, "Then to the Gentiles also God has granted **repentance** (change of direction) **that leads to life**." Even though repentance means any type of change, good or bad, the only type of change (repentance) that leads to life is turning towards Jesus and putting our trust in Jesus instead of the law as your source of salvation. In this verse, God gave the Gentiles the opportunity to turn towards God. Prior to Jesus, the Jews had the Law, and the gentiles had their idols.

Then we have **Acts 17:30 (ESV)**, where it says, "The times of ignorance God overlooked, but now he commands all people everywhere to **repent**" (change direction). God overlooks our ignorance, just like He overlooked Paul when Paul thought he was doing the right thing by killing Christians. Especially, since it was God Himself who created us and being ignorant is a natural byproduct of being human. We certainly can't make ourselves ignorant. It's not like you wake up and think to yourself "yeah, I want to be a dumb ass today. What can I do to turn myself into an idiot?"

In **Acts 20:21 (ESV)** it says, "testifying both to Jews and to Greeks of **repentance** toward God and of faith in our Lord Jesus Christ". In other words, to turn around and go towards God and faith in Jesus. You are still turning away from something when you turn around and walk towards God.

Even though we are turning away from our old belief system of putting our trust in the Law as the way that leads to salvation, a lot of people still think we need to repent of our sins, but that's NOT true. The Bible **DOES NOT** say that. The Bible clearly says to repent **FOR** the forgiveness of sins. The bottom line is it is impossible to turn towards God and trust in Jesus and also believe and trust in the Law at the same time. We have to pick one. In order to turn towards Jesus, we have to turn around and walk away from the Law.

Earlier I mentioned that repentance has nothing to do with regret or being remorseful. Here is an example in **II Corinthians 7:10 (ESV)** of what I was talking about, "For Godly grief produces a **repentance** that leads to salvation without regret, whereas worldly grief produces death". Take notice that Godly grief produces repentance without **REGRET**.

Here we see a different use of repentance in **Acts 8 (ESV)**, where Philip is preaching in Samaria, and many believed and were baptized including Simon the magician. However, those who believed had not received the Holy Spirit yet. So, when the apostles in Jerusalem heard that so many believed and were baptized, they sent John and Peter to go pray over them that they would receive the Holy Spirit. When Simon the magician saw that John

REPENTANCE

and Peter were laying on their hands and the believers were receiving the Holy Spirit, Simon, being an opportunist and wanting to get in on the action, offered to pay John and Peter money to receive this gift of the laying on of the hands so he can give the Holy Spirit as well. Don't get me wrong, there's nothing wrong with being an opportunist, it's just that Simon the magician's heart was not in the right place. Then Peter said to Simon in v22, "Repent, therefore, of this wickedness of yours, and pray to the Lord that, if possible, the intent of your heart may be forgiven you".

In this account in **Acts 8 (ESV)**, Peter says to repent of this wickedness. Basically, he is telling Simon to turn away from his wickedness. The context is completely different than the scriptures talking about turning to God for the forgiveness of sins. Simon had already repented and turned towards Jesus. But yet he still had his old behavior patterns as we all do. Although, some people may interpret this to mean that we are all wicked and need to turn away from wickedness or our sin. That's not what it's saying. This is an isolated situation that happened only once when dealing with Simon the magician. When Peter told him to turn away from his wickedness, the translators used the word repent, since the definition of repent is to turn around, and walk away or make a change. Simon had already repented and turned towards Jesus, so repentance in this situation was just

Peter telling him to rethink his attitude and don't use God for personal gain.

There are many applications of the word repent in the Bible, but nowhere do we see that we are to repent of our sins. But whatever we are doing at the moment, the word repent means to change direction or change our mind about something, regardless of the context. However, when the Bible says to repent (turn around) and move towards Jesus for the forgiveness of sins, it is **NOT** talking about repenting of our sins. Because it's too late, we have already sinned and we're already facing a death sentence, and we can't just undo that. Even if we could repent of previous sins, we still have our human behavior patterns. And we all fall short of the Glory of God. Besides, Jesus already took care of all sin for us. And God does not give us much of a choice. We are stuck with our back against the wall and Jesus is the only way out. If we repent, turn around towards Him, He **WILL** forgive us of our sins and let us go free.

As you can see, repentance has nothing to do with having regret or being remorseful. The Bible says to turn towards God **FOR** the forgiveness of sins...period. It never mentions begging for forgiveness or being remorseful or feeling regret. It is simply an Old English word that the translators used that means to change our mind or turn around. So, if we turn to Jesus for salvation and turn away from the Law we have repented. But, if we move away from God and start worshiping Satan, we have also repented. However, the only repentance that leads to life is repentance toward God.

Then, the next thing that happens is we receive the Holy Spirt. We saw earlier in **Acts 2:38 (ESV)**, where Peter says, "Repent and be baptized every one of you in the name of Jesus Christ **FOR** the forgiveness of your sins, and you will **receive the gift of the Holy Spirit**". Once we repent and turn toward Jesus, we will receive the Holy Spirt. It is a gift. What is this Holy Spirit and how is it tied to baptism? We will explore these biblical concepts in the next section.

BAPTISM, HOLY SPIRIT, AND FIRE

*L*et's take a look at Baptism, the Holy Spirit and Fire for a minute. You might be thinking what do these three things have to do with each other? Although, Baptism and the Holy spirit sound like they go together. In fact, we just read that we should repent and be baptized, then we will receive the Holy spirit. These two events seem to go together, but Fire seems to be out of place. What could it mean? Let's take a look and see what we can find out.

First of all, the word Baptize, or Baptism is such a strange word. It's not even used in modern English. The only time you hear that word is in religious settings or in connection with the Bible. That's why, to a lot of people, it sounds very religious, but it's **NOT**. It's just another one of those Old English words that the translators used when they were translating the New Testament from Greek to English. The word Baptize simply means to immerse, which was briefly mentioned earlier as well.

So, where did this idea of Baptizing come from? This ritual of immersion and what are people getting immersed into? Was John the Baptist as a teenager playing around the pool with his friends and one of them pushed another into the pool as a joke and while the rest of them were laughing, John spoke up and said, "oh man, he got you good, you were totally baptized". Then John thought to himself..." Hmm, that's what I need to do, I need to go around and start Baptizing people". No, that's not exactly how things happened.

It started with an Angel from God. Zechariah and his wife Elizabeth (Lizzy as I like to call her) did not have children, so Zechariah prayed to God that He would bless them with children, but it wasn't until they were too old to have children that God decided to bless them. Wow! Isn't that just like God to wait until the most inconvenient time and then out of nowhere...**Boom!**

So, in **Luke 1:13-17 (ESV)**, we see that the Angel of God appears to Zechariah. It says in v13 "But the angel said to him, "Do not be afraid, Zechariah, for your prayer has been heard, and your wife Elizabeth will bear you a son, and you shall call his name John. v14 And, you will have joy and gladness, and many will rejoice at his birth, v15 for he will be great before the Lord. And he must not drink wine or strong drink, and he will be filled with the Holy Spirit, even from his mother's womb. v16 And, he will turn many of the children of Israel to the Lord their God, v17 and he will go before him, in the spirit and power of Elijah, to turn the hearts of the fathers to the children, and the disobedient to the wisdom of the just, to make ready for the Lord, a people prepared".

Not only did God bless Zechariah & Lizzy with a child, but He also had a plan for John. His job in v16 was to turn many of the children of Israel towards God and in v17 he was to do this "before him". Who is "him"? We know from subsequent scriptures that shortly after John was out doing his thing that Jesus arrived on the scene. So, when v17 says before Him it's referring to: before Jesus arrived. Then further in v17 it clarifies it a little more and says to make ready for the Lord, a people prepared. In other words, John is preparing the way for Jesus.

Let's notice a couple of things. First of all, be careful of what you ask for, you might end up pregnant at an old age. Second, John the Baptist was part of God's original plan from the beginning, but God was waiting until the right moment. Keep in mind that when your destiny is part of God's purpose or plan, **you don't get a choice**! We like to think we are in charge and that we are the master of our sea because we have free choice. However, from the many examples in the Bible, you can see that we have free choice about our behavior, but not about God's purpose or plan to save the world.

God created man with an expiration date and that is part of our destiny to eventually expire. We have no choice over that. And, when God has a plan or a job for us, before we expire, we don't get a choice about that either. Oh sure, we have free choice, and we can try to refuse, but you see what happened to Jonah when he refused. The same goes for John the Baptist. He did not get a choice about his destiny. God "planned" on John being the forerunner to Jesus, long before he was born, then after John fulfilled his purpose, he would expire (die). Not only that, God did not wait for John to believe and come to Him, He gave him the holy spirit before he was born without him even being a willing participant. He had no choice. It was already decided before he was born.

The Prophet Isaiah prophesied long ago about John the Baptist in **Isaiah 40:3 (ESV)**, where it says, "A voice cries in the wilderness 'prepare the way of the LORD; make straight in the desert a highway for our God'". God decided on John's purpose, his job, long before he was born.

Then in **Matthew 3:1-3 (ESV)**, Matthew was writing about John when he made a reference to Isaiah's prophesy, v1 "In those days, John the Baptist came preaching in the wilderness of Judea, v2 "Repent, for the kingdom of heaven is at hand." Then Matthew said in v3 "For this is he who was spoken of by the prophet Isaiah when he said, "The voice of one crying in the wilderness: 'Prepare the way of the Lord; make his paths straight'". As you can see, that was part of the plan from the beginning.

Then, continuing in **Matthew 3:11 (ESV)**, we see Matthew quoting John as he was preaching in the wilderness, when he said "I baptize you with water for repentance, but he who is coming after me is mightier than I, whose sandals I am not worthy to carry. He will baptize you with the Holy Spirit and Fire".

Basically, John was explaining that he immerses them in water, but when Jesus arrives, He will immerse them in the Holy Spirit and Fire. We understand the Holy Spirit part. There are plenty of examples in Acts and elsewhere to explain the Holy Spirit. But, what in the world does John mean when he says, He will baptize (immerse) you with fire?

You can't just assume every time fire is mentioned in the Bible that it's talking about something bad or about Hell Fire. For one, we've already discovered that the fiery pit Jesus mentioned a number of times earlier was Gehenna, the garbage dump, just outside of Jerusalem. And two, aside from the fiery garbage pit, we can't find any evidence or any scriptures that support an eternal existence for sinners in a fiery pit. The only clear Biblical evidence of what happens to sinners is: the wages of sin is death. So, what does John mean when he says Jesus will baptize (immerse) you with fire? Well, it is not clear, so we can't just assume.

However, in **Acts 2:1-3 (ESV)**, we see that the Holy Spirit got poured out on the day of Pentecost and divided tongues of **Fire** would appear. Is that what John was talking about? He doesn't say! Here is what it says in v1 "When the day of Pentecost arrived, they were all together in one place. v2 And, suddenly there came from heaven a sound like a mighty rushing wind, and it filled the entire house where they were sitting. v3 And, divided tongues as of **Fire** appeared to them and rested on each one of them".

Fire is used several times in the Bible as an analogy of how a silversmith or goldsmith might use fire to refine and purify just like it says in **Malachi 3:2-3 (ESV)**. This example is referring to Jesus that He is like a refiner's fire, and He will purify the sons of Levi. Could John be referring to fire symbolically that Jesus would Baptize (immerse) them with the Holy Spirit and then fire for purification? He doesn't explain! Here is what **Malachi 3 (ESV)** says, v2 "But who can endure the day of his coming, and who can stand when he appears? For he is like a refiner's fire and like fullers' soap. v3 He will sit as a refiner and purifier of silver, and he will purify the sons of Levi and refine them like gold and silver, and they will bring offerings in righteousness to the Lord".

Whether John was talking about the divided tongues of fire that would soon appear on the day of Pentecost or if he was talking about a cleansing / purifying fire, you can see in **Matthew 3:11 (ESV)**, that John was talking to one group of people, the same group of people that had already repented and was already baptized by water. Then John said to that group, that He (Jesus) would baptize **YOU**, that same group, with the Holy Spirit and Fire. The one group of people he referred to as **YOU** would get baptized with **both** the Holy Spirit **AND** Fire. He did not say either the Holy Spirit **OR** Fire. He said **AND** fire. So, whatever this **Fire** was, it was a good thing. And it was waiting for those who believe, the ones that have already repented. Here is where God starts to add people to the team of believers.

Then as John continued from **Matthew 3:11 (ESV)** into v12, where it says, "His winnowing fork is in his hand, and he will clear his threshing floor and gather his wheat into the barn, but the chaff he will burn with unquenchable fire". What is John the Baptist talking about here? And what is the reference about wheat going into the barn and the chaff going into the fire?

A lot of biblical commentaries as well as some Christian beliefs say this is an analogy about Jesus separating the believers from the unbelievers. Whereas the unbelievers will get burned up in the unquenchable fire, which they consider to be Hell or the Lake of Fire. However, **NO WHERE** in that scripture does it say that! The Churches and Commentaries are just assuming that. And you can quote me on that! This is only an analogy. By the way, here's a fun fact. A winnowing fork is like a pitchfork. In the meantime, let's explore this analogy a little closer.

Think about the timeframe for a minute. First of all, this was at a time when John the Baptist first started recruiting for the team of believers. These were new recruits that just got baptized by water. None of them had met Jesus yet, and John the Baptist, the team coach, had not yet met Him in person either. The concept of salvation by Jesus, salvation by grace was unknown and not clearly understood yet. Not only that, but we also saw earlier that the concept of Hell did not exist at that time either. It was never mentioned in the Old Testament and their religious beliefs did not include the concept of Hell. It doesn't add up that John the Baptist would give such a vague and mysterious analogy even before salvation by Jesus was a thing. Not only that, but none of these new recruits even asked him "what are you talking about, bro". That's because the analogy wasn't so vague and mysterious to them. They were farmers and knew exactly what he was talking about. So, I decided to do a little research on my own.

In the process of researching this, I learned some things about wheat I never knew. Probably more than I wanted to know. The first thing I found out is that threshing is the process of separating the wheat from the stalk, which was done on a flat service, typically called the threshing floor. Another thing I didn't know was that wheat has a husk, similar to a corn husk, but much smaller. This miniature husk is called the chaff, which is the useless or unusable part of the wheat. Then if we go back to **Matthew 3:11 (ESV)**, we see, once again, that John was talking to the new recruits, the group of people that have already repented, when he starts talking in v12 about the wheat and chaff. So, if the wheat represents believers and the chaff is the useless or unusable part of the wheat, then John is saying that Jesus will separate the usable parts from the unusable parts of the believers. This is another way to say that Jesus will purify or cleanse us of our sin and take away the unusable / bad parts and burn them. Perhaps like a dermatologist might burn off a mole. It has nothing to do with separating the believers from the unbelievers and sending the unbelievers to Hell or Lake of Fire. A stalk of wheat is **ONE** stalk with both good parts and unusable parts.

Also, the reference to an unquenchable fire **DOES NOT** mean Hell. Gehenna garbage dump was considered unquenchable fire, since the fire never died out, due to garbage piling up every day. We can't just assume fire or unquenchable fire always means Hell, especially since there's nothing in these scriptures that talks about Hell. Besides, the concept of Hell **DID NOT** exist at that time, based on what we discovered earlier in the scriptures.

Prior to the day of Pentecost in Acts, John was out there baptizing (immersing) people with water, which was symbolic of the baptism (immersion) with the Holy Spirit that will come later by Jesus.

Then if we fast forward to the Gospel of John (not John the Baptist), we see that John would record the events and conversations by writing them down. In **John 14 (ESV)**, Jesus is having a serious talk with his Disciples. He is starting to say his goodbyes. This is troubling to His Disciples who have been His brothers for more than three years at this point. These were His friends. Jesus said He was going to His Father's house and prepare a place for them and then come back to get them. Then he tells them, they already know how to get there.

In the typical vague and mysterious style of Jesus, He just confused the crap out of them. So, Thomas spoke up and said serious bro, how are we supposed to know how to get there when we don't even know where you're going? Then in v6, Jesus said to him, "**I am the way, and the truth, and the life**. No one comes to the Father except through me". Then, Philip, still confused, says show us the Father and that's good enough for us. Then Jesus comes back and says Dude, it doesn't work that way. Anyone who's seen me HAS seen the Father, I am just like Him. I am in the Father and the Father is in me.

Then, in **John 14:15-17 (ESV)**, Jesus says v15 "If you love me, you will keep my commandments. v16 And I will ask the Father, and he will give you another Helper, to be with you forever, v17 even the **Spirit of truth**, whom the world cannot receive, because it neither sees him nor knows him. **You know Him**, for He **dwells with you and will be in you**".

Since Jesus is the way and the truth, in the flesh, and the Helper is the Spirit of Truth, then this Helper, this Spirit of Truth, appears to be the spirit form of the Truth. And, since Jesus says He is the truth. Then, Jesus must be the Helper, the spirit of truth.

Jesus also says in v17 that the disciples know the spirit of truth, and this Spirit of Truth, this Helper **dwells with them and will be in them**. Who dwells with them? **Jesus does!** Jesus dwells with them and in v6 Jesus is the truth in the flesh and the Helper is the spirit of that truth. Then in v16 it says the Father will send another Helper. Another Helper is basically the same Helper (Jesus) as before, but in another form. This time the Helper (Jesus) will come in a spiritual form.

Then in v18-21, Jesus is saying he's physically leaving, so the world won't be able to see him, but we will be able to see him and because Jesus lives, we will live also. Then Jesus goes on to say in v20, "In that day you will know that **I am in my Father, and you in me, and I in you**". Then in v21, Jesus is talking about us being loved by the Father and if the Father loves us, Jesus is saying He will love us too and manifest himself to us. How is He going to do that? The other Judas (not Iscariot) asked the same thing in v22. Jesus was clear that He is the Helper (Comforter), the Spirit of Truth. No one got confused about that. The only thing that was confusing to Judas was **HOW**.

Then in **John 14:25-26 (ESV)**, it says v25 "These things I have spoken to you while I am still with you. v26 But the Helper, **the Holy Spirit**, whom the **Father will send in my name**, he will teach you all things and bring to your remembrance all that I have said to you". Here we see the Helper referred to as the Holy Spirit and since Jesus is the truth, the Spirit of Truth, and the Helper, then Jesus must also be the Holy Spirit. In other words, the Holy Spirit is the Spirit form of Jesus Christ.

Let's summarize John 14 for a minute:

1. Jesus says He is the Truth **(John 14:6)**

2. Jesus said Another Helper is the Spirit of Truth **(John 14:17)**

3. If Jesus is the Truth and Another Helper is the Spirit of Truth, then another Helper is the spirit of Jesus. Basically, Jesus in the spirit form.

4. Jesus said The Spirit of Truth dwells with you **(John 14:17)**

5. Jesus is the Truth in the flesh, and He dwelled with them. Another way of saying Jesus is the Spirit of Truth...the truth in spirit form.

6. Jesus said the Spirit of Truth will dwell in you **(John 14:17)**

7. Jesus will be in us **(John 14:20)**

8. Jesus must be the Spirit of Truth since He will be in us and the Spirit of Truth also dwells in us.

9. Jesus said the Helper is the Holy Spirit **(John 14:26)**

10. And, since the Helper is the Spirit of Truth, Jesus in the spirit form, and now we see the Helper is also the Holy Spirit, then Jesus must be the Holy Spirit, the Helper, and the Spirit of Truth.

Now let's take a look at the Day of Pentecost. The word Pentecost literally means to count 50, but what are they counting? The Day of Pentecost was the first time they were covered by the Holy Spirit, basically baptized by the Holy Spirit. According to Jewish custom, as instructed by God in the Old Testament, they would count 50 days from the 1st holy day after Passover, which is the 1st day of unleavened bread, and they would end up on the Day of Pentecost.

Now here we are on the Day of Pentecost in **Acts 2:1-4 (ESV)** where the Holy Spirit is poured out. After Jesus was killed, he stayed dead in the grave for 3 days. Then, He was resurrected, but He didn't immediately go to Heaven. He showed up in His new spirit form and appeared just like that to His crew, His disciples. And He stayed with them for 40 days talking about the gospel (good news) of the Kingdom of God.

After that, He ascended to Heaven. Then, once He was gone, about a week later, we get to the Day of Pentecost. And, in **Acts 2:1-4 (ESV)**, it says "When the day of Pentecost arrived, they were all together in one place. v2 And, suddenly there came from heaven a sound like a mighty rushing wind, and it filled the entire house where they were sitting. v3 And, divided tongues as of fire appeared to them and rested on each one of them. v4 And, they were all filled with the Holy Spirit and began to speak in other tongues as the Spirit gave them utterance".

Wow! That must have been powerful. Here you see them getting baptized (immersed) with the Holy Spirit and you see the tongues of fire as mentioned earlier. In v1 it said, "they were all together", but who are "they" and how many are there? It would make sense that "**they**" are the same group that John the Baptist dunked in water and told them that later Jesus would cover them with the Holy Spirit. And, in **Acts 1 (ESV)**, it looks like 120 of them were having a Church meeting and voting on a new disciple to replace Judas Iscariot when suddenly the Holy Spirit arrived. The sound of the Holy Spirit was so disruptive that the entire town showed up to see what was happening. That's when Peter started preaching. Then after his sermon, in **Acts 2:42 (ESV)**, it looks like three thousand more were baptized by receiving the Holy Spirit.

We talked about Baptism with the Holy Spirit in which Jesus previously said the Father would send a Comforter, a Helper, which we now know is Jesus Christ in the Spirit form. We also know that John the Baptist said Jesus would Baptize with the Holy Spirit, so those who believe will be immersed in, dunked by, covered with, and filled up with the Holy Spirit. However, we briefly touched on the subject of Fire earlier, but let's revisit it for a minute.

In the Old Testament, the food offering / burnt offering were animal sacrifices cooked by Fire. In Leviticus 23:18, Numbers 28:13,24, Numbers 29:6, 13, God described the burning of sacrificial meat with fire as "a soothing aroma to the LORD". They could have just brought the dead lamb, swung it up there on the alter and said here ya go God, but instead they decided to cook it with fire. A dead lamb as it decays stinks to high heaven, but as you cook it with fire, the aroma permeates the air, which excites the taste buds as you anticipate the flavor. Fire makes things a lot better. Grilled burgers taste a lot better than raw burgers.

Then, if we look in **Zechariah 12 (ESV)**, we see a time when all the nations will rise up against Jerusalem and they will rise up against Judah as well. This is a prophesy of the end time as we will see later in Revelation. But what does all this have to do with Fire? We will get to that in a few minutes. In the meantime, in v7-9 we read, "And the Lord will give salvation to the tents of Judah first, that the glory of the house of David and the glory of the inhabitants of Jerusalem may not surpass that of Judah. v8 On that day the Lord will protect the inhabitants of Jerusalem, so that the feeblest among them on that day shall be like David, and the house of David shall be like God, like the angel of the Lord, going before them. v9 And, on that day I will seek to destroy all the nations that come against Jerusalem".

Here we see a couple of things. God will give salvation to Judah first. Once again, we see God doing everything in order...Judah is first. Besides, who and what is Judah? Earlier we talked about Abraham, Isaac, and Jacob. Jacob's name was later changed to Israel. As you probably figured by now, the country Israel was named after him. Then, Israel had 12 sons, in which we touched on earlier regarding the 12 tribes of Israel. Well, Judah was one of his sons, one of the tribes. The southern region of the country Israel was named after Judah. It includes the cities of Jerusalem and Bethlehem. Also, that's where Jews originally came from. Normally, you think Israel, but more specifically the region of Judah. The word Jew was actually derived phonetically from the name **Ju**-dah. So, when Zechariah says God will give salvation to Judah first, he is saying God is going to save the Jews first.

In those days, prior to Jesus and the New Covenant, the Jews were considered God's people. Later, those who received Christ would be considered God's people. Symbolically, you can say those who receive Christ would be "spiritual Jews". So, when Zechariah prophesied that God would save Judah first, he didn't fully understand the magnitude of Jesus' arrival and His impact on salvation.

However, now we know that those who receive Christ, those who believe will be saved first. They are the First Fruits. So that makes sense, the Jews used to be considered God's people, but now, with the New Covenant, those who are born again and receive Christ are God's people. Since God saves Judah (spiritual Jews) first, then who does He save next? God does everything in order.

In Zechariah, he keeps referring to "On That Day", which indicates the end times. Then in **Zechariah 13:1 (ESV)**, the prophesy continues "On that day there shall be a fountain opened for the house of David and the inhabitants of Jerusalem, to cleanse them from sin and uncleanness". Now, this fountain will cleanse them (us) from sin and uncleanness. And we know that Jesus will cleanse us and since we learned that the Holy Spirit is the spirit form of Jesus, it's the Holy Spirit in us that cleanses us from sin.

So, if we jump to **Zechariah 13:7-9 (ESV)** it prophesies more of the end time. It says v7 "Awake, O sword, against my shepherd, against the man who stands next to me, declares the Lord of hosts". Strike the shepherd, and the sheep will be scattered; I will turn my hand against the little ones. v8 In the whole land, declares the Lord, two thirds shall be cut off and perish, and one third shall be left alive". It sounds like Zechariah is talking about the end times.

Then in v9, he says "And I will put this third **into the fire**, and refine them as one refines silver, and test them as gold is tested. They will call upon my name, and I will answer them. I will say, 'They are my people'; and they will say, 'The Lord is my God'". **Wait!** Here we see that the surviving one-third will be tossed **into the fire**. Just like we will see later about those thrown into the Lake of Fire. Then they will call upon the name of the Lord and God calls them His people. What happens after they are tossed into the fire? They will call upon the name of the Lord and He will call them His people. This fire was not some kind of punishment or Hell, it was for the purpose of refining them and testing them like gold and silver. You would think that the fire would burn them up, but it didn't. In this case, it was symbolic and used as an analogy in the process of cleansing and purifying God's people.

This was all part of God's plan laid out in the beginning, way ahead of time. He does not give them a choice when He throws them into the fire. But when they all get out of the fire, everyone decided on their own to call upon the name of the Lord. That's everyone. Did He force them to call on His name? NO! They wanted to. Once God gets through with everyone, every knee will bow and every tongue will call upon His name. Not because God forces them, but because they will want to. God wins in the end!

You saw a similar analogy earlier in **Malachi 3:2-3 (ESV)** in which fire was used to refine and purify.

Basically, in the Bible, you see Fire used as a metaphor or a symbol to demonstrate the process that God uses to purify or burn off sin and cleanse us. Once we believe in Jesus and we're Baptized with the Holy Spirit, it doesn't mean that all of our issues suddenly disappear. God uses trials and tests to refine us like the silversmith uses fire. And God uses fire to bring us to repentance in the first place.

For instance, Peter refers to trials as fiery trials in **I Peter 4:12 (ESV)** where it says, "Beloved, do not be surprised at the fiery trial when it comes upon you to test you, as though something strange were happening to you". And he mentions we will be tested by Fire in **I peter 1:6-7 (ESV)**, where it says, v6 "In this you rejoice, though now for a little while, if necessary, you have been grieved by various trials, v7 so that the tested genuineness of your faith—more precious than gold that perishes though it is tested by fire—may be found to result in praise and glory and honor at the revelation of Jesus Christ".

We also see in **I Corinthians 3 (ESV)** where Paul is writing to the Church at Corinth, explaining that Christ is the foundation of the Church. At that time, the Corinthians were new Christians. Some of them were following one pastor and some were following another. It's okay to have a favorite pastor, but what Paul was explaining to them is that Christ is the foundation of the Church and both pastors work for Him. Sometimes, we have that same issue today, where some will put their trust in the pastor rather than in God.

Then Paul explains that he did the planting by sending Apollos (the pastor) and Apollos did the watering. But it is God who does the growing. Basically, telling them to put your trust in God and not a man. Take a look at **I Corinthians 3: 6-7 (ESV)** where it says "I planted, Apollos watered, but God gave the growth. v7 So neither he who plants, nor he who waters is anything, but only God who gives the growth". Take note that it is **ONLY** God who gives growth. This is where your brain goes "yeah but". Yeah, but what? Yeah, but we have to overcome, right? NO! That is a very clear statement..." but only God who gives the growth". It is our job to do nothing, except put our trust in God and He will give us growth. However, the work we do now is not related to building righteousness or overcoming. The foundation of Jesus Christ is already built. Our work now is a work of faith, which is putting our trust in God. Then our work of faith will get added to the foundation of Jesus that is already in place.

Then in **I Corinthians 3:12-15 (ESV)** Paul explains what happens to our work of faith as we build upon the foundation. V12 "Now if anyone builds on the foundation with gold, silver, precious stones, wood, hay, straw— v13 each one's work will become manifest, for the Day will disclose it, because it will be revealed by fire, and the fire will test what sort of work each one has done. v14 If the work that anyone has built on the foundation survives, he will receive a reward. v15 If anyone's work is burned up, he will suffer loss, **though he himself will be saved**, but only as through fire"

Take a look at that for a minute. If your works don't survive the test of fire, they get burned up. **Wow! This is interesting!** It's the works that get burned up, **not the person** who had the counterfeit works. The person himself **will be saved**, but only by going through the fire as mentioned in verse 15. Our works will be revealed by fire.

The analogy of fire is used as a tool to prove or reveal if your works of faith are real or fake. Just like Gold or Silver. It's also used as a refining tool to burn off the unusable parts or any blemishes. This process sounds like the infamous Lake of Fire we will hear about in Revelation. The works of those thrown into the Lake of Fire will get burned up, but **he himself will be saved** as Paul mentioned. Just like we saw in Zechariah where those who were thrown into the fire came out calling upon the name of the Lord.

Basically, this is the same thing Peter mentioned above, in **I peter 1:6-7 (ESV)**, where he says, v6 "In this you rejoice, though now for a little while, if necessary, you have been grieved by various trials, v7 so that the **tested genuineness of your faith**—more precious than gold that perishes though it is tested by fire". It is your faith / works of faith that gets tested.

As you can see, the Bible uses the analogy of fire as a tool to cleanse and purify as well as a way to burn up or burn off unusable parts. So, when we are baptized /

immersed with the Holy Spirit, we still go through trials / trials of fire to cleanse us, strengthen us, and get us ready for Jesus.

Now it's time for another recap...

1. We see that God created man after the God kind, in His image. God is starting a family. Jesus called Him father and us brothers. And, we are God's children, His babies. God created man to reproduce himself, just like God is reproducing Himself through man.

2. We also see that God is a planner, a designer. He designed Noah's Ark. He planned on Jesus' sacrifice long before He created man. He designed man with all of our feelings, emotions, and human nature. He planned and directed the life of Ruth all the way through her generations down to David and then directed his life all the way down to Mary, so that Jesus could be born. Now that's a plan that requires a lot of work and patience. Every detail had to fall into place just right.

3. We also see all the people God worked with to make His plan come together, such as Noah, Abraham, Isaac, Jacob, Moses, David, John the Baptist, and many others. If anything changed or didn't go as planned, it would ruin His entire plan. There is no

room for error! Not even free choice is going to get in the way of God making His plan happen.

4. It is God's plan, God's purpose, God's will. He has to direct every detail to get to His endgame. Just like a movie director directs every detail on a movie set to make sure a movie gets completed properly.

5. God does not leave anything to chance. Everything is well planned out. He does not have "Oh Crap" moments or "Whoops-a-Daisy!" moments or "Ah man, I lost another one" moments. God **DOES NOT LOSE!** He has a plan, and everything has to work together to fit into that plan.

6. Remember, when God created man, Satan had already rebelled. Then He put man down here with Satan. This was no accident. God knew what He was doing. It was intentional. God was completely on top of the situation just like He was with Job. God is always in control.

7. Then, God created a process in which a human child is born through a birthing process. Not only that, Jesus introduces the concept of being born again, which is also a birthing process. This was **NO** coincidence. It was all part of God's plan.

8. Then, when a child is born, does that child get a choice about being born? NO! Then why do some people think that God gives us a choice about being born again? And when God comes to us and starts to show us His way is best and we start to kick and put up a fight, just like a child in the womb, is God going to abort us? Are some of us just too strong for God to handle, so He just gives up on us? What if your child is kicking and fighting in the womb and refuses to come out? Are you going to abort your child and say forget about it, he's too much trouble? Of course not! Then, why do some people think God is going to throw in the towel and abort some of His children?

9. Even though we have free choice about our behavior, whether or not to put on a coat when it's cold or the 1,000 other decisions we have to make on a daily basis, we don't get a choice about everything. We are living within the framework of God's plan and we don't have a choice.

10. Besides, God's plan is **NOT** about choice, it's about God having a plan from the beginning. And God following through with His plan and finishing what He started. Once God does His part and finishes His job, then our answer, our choice will always be YES. That is God's End Game. Just like I convinced my

friends to say YES to pizza. God started out with a winning plan, but if He doesn't finish the job, then God loses. Which wouldn't make sense anyway since **GOD DOES NOT LOSE!**

11. We saw in the Bible that Jesus paid the price for **ALL** sin, for the entire world, for everyone. We also saw that God's will is that **ALL** should reach repentance, that's everyone. And we read that Jesus came to destroy the works of the devil. The works of the devil would be Sin and Death, leaving Satan with nothing.

12. We also found out from the scriptures that no one goes to Heaven when they die. We all go to the grave. Even David, a man after God's own heart is still in the tomb. We came from dust, and we return to dust. No different than any other creature.

13. We also discovered that there is no such thing as an immortal soul. The word soul simply means creature or living creature. And we learned that Jesus is the only one with immortality.

14. We also discovered that the Old English word Hell means to cover and conceal. And nowhere in the Old Testament does it mention a fiery pit where sinners go when they die. The word Hell only shows

up in some translations when the translators were trying to find an English word to best describe Abode of the Dead, a pit, or the grave.

15. Then, of course, we searched the New Testament and found that Jesus talked about Hell, but He was referring to Gehenna (Valley of Hinnom), the fiery garbage dump outside of Jerusalem. Again, this was an Old English word the translators used in the early 1600's to try to describe the Gehenna fire near Jerusalem. Nowhere in any of the original Greek texts of the New Testament can you find any kind of fiery pit of punishment where sinners go when they die. God is certainly capable of expressing himself, so if Hell was such a big deal, then why didn't He just say it. Something else interesting is that Paul, who wrote to multiple Churches, and he wrote most of the New Testament, never once talked about Hell.

16. Then we came to understand that the translators used another Old English word repent or repentance, which simply means to turn around, change direction, change your mind, or change your beliefs. It has nothing to do with repenting of sin or being remorseful. Too late for that, we have all sinned and fall short of the glory of God. Repenting is to turn around and start walking towards God. To

turn away from putting your trust in the law and start putting your trust in Jesus as the source of our salvation.

17. Then we learned that Jesus would die a physical death and pay the price for the sins of the world and three days later he was resurrected. Then He would baptize / immerse us with the Holy Spirt. And we learned that Jesus himself, in the spirit form, is the Holy Spirit.

18. We also learned that fire was a word used symbolically to describe the method in which God uses to refine and purify us and a way to make us clean. Just like a goldsmith refines gold.

Some of this information may be new, and some of it may differ from what you've heard or been taught. However, as you can see, God came up with a plan and a purpose long before He created man. And He included man as part of that plan. You can see God's plan outlined right there in your Bible. However, you might be thinking, if everything is that easy, that black and white, then what about the wrath of God, the day of the Lord, and the day of judgment?

Well, God's judgment does sound ominous, and it sounds harsh. Where is God's mercy during this time of judgment? Does God compartmentalize and throw mercy out the window? Does God have a split personality? Is He bi-polar? Laying down the law one minute and full of mercy the next? Why did God go to all this trouble of coming up with a long-term plan, which included the sacrifice of Jesus, just to lose in the end? All those people for which Jesus died, just lost, all in one day of judgment? Is God going to say to Jesus, well we tried, but you can't win them all? **WHO DO YOU THINK GOD IS?** God always wins! Do you think God is that weak that He couldn't save everyone? Do you think His plan was flawed from the beginning and God failed? Or do you think God came up with a losing game-plan intentionally? Do you think Jesus' time on earth, His death, and resurrection was a waste of time? I don't think so!

So, let's take a closer look at the judgment of God and what the Bible says about it...

JUDGMENT

There are a lot of assumptions that come to mind when we hear the word judgment in the Bible. It congers up certain images in our head. I used to think it meant sentencing to death, hell, or the lake of fire. Sometimes we think it's where God finally gets fed up, stomps His foot, and says, "that's it, I'm done with all of you stubborn humans, you can all go to Hell for all I care". That's assuming God is **NOT** able to mold stubborn clay. What is the clay supposed to do if the potter walks away? Can the clay mold itself? Of course not.

    These are all just assumptions, since most of the scriptures in the Bible about judgment never tells us what judgment means. Until I came across the one scripture in the Bible that defines judgment right there in **John 3:18-20 (ESV)**, where it says in v18 "Whoever believes in him is not condemned, but whoever does not believe is condemned already, because he has not believed in the name of the only Son of God. v19 And, this is the judgment: the light has come into the world, and people loved the darkness rather than the light because their works were evil. v20 For, everyone who does wicked things hates the light and does not come to the light, lest his works should be exposed".

Here we notice a few things. One, whoever is in the group that includes those who believe are not condemned, not found guilty. Then, those in the other group, who don't believe, who were already guilty, will stay where they are as part of the guilty group. Remember, we all started out as one big group of guilty people. We all fall short of the glory of God. Then God came along and started putting us into two groups: The believers and the unbelievers, guilty and not guilty. Whereas the not guilty can move to the front of the line and the guilty stays where they are. This is **NOT** punishment or God sentencing us to death for our sins. God is just separating us into two different groups.

It actually tells you what Judgment is, right there in verse 19. This is the only scripture in the Bible that I found that tells us what judgment means. It says, v19 "**this is the judgment:**". What is the judgment? "Light came and people loved darkness rather than light". How is this the judgment? In verse 20 you can see that the light exposes the works of everyone who does wicked, so they stay away from the light. This has nothing to do with punishment or sentencing, the judgment is just the method of exposing those who have wicked works, wicked deeds. It's the way of determining who is guilty and who is not guilty. The light is the method of separating the good works from the evil works.

We've seen this throughout the Bible. God separates everyone into two groups, two teams. The guilty and the not guilty, the condemned and the ones no longer condemned, the believer and the unbeliever, the ones with evil works and the ones with good works. We also see that God has two harvests, the first fruits and then the ingathering (rest of the crop) and He has the two resurrections...the first fruits and the rest of the people.

In this case, the light exposes those who have wicked works. Notice very carefully that it is the **works that are evil and not the person who is doing the evil works**. God did not create humans evil or wicked. And humans cannot become something different than how God created us, which is human. However, God did create humans with the capacity to do wicked things, but that doesn't make them evil. So, when v20 above says the light exposes the works of everyone who does wickedness, not the person.

Basically, judgment is where the light exposes those hiding in the shadows to avoid having their evil deeds, their evil works exposed by the light. Judgment is not punishment or sentencing. It's when those who do evil deeds are exposed / found guilty.

I picture it like this: A man robs a bank and takes you hostage. Soon, day turns into night. A manhunt ensues. The police bring out their helicopter with the big spotlight.

You're waiting for your chance to escape your captor. As the helicopter gets closer you can see the spotlight. Then your captor gets distracted, so you make a run for it. You run towards the light yelling here I am, here I am, save me. Just like you would yell out to Jesus...here I am, save me. You have nothing to hide, so you embrace the light, yelling save me. However, the bank robber slithers into the darkness, into the shadows hiding from the light. He eventually gets caught and found guilty, but he has not been sentenced yet. That comes later.

The good news for him is that Jesus already paid the price for his crime, even though he was found guilty. So, the bank robber gets to go free. The judge says, "This is your lucky day, someone already went to jail for you, so you get to go free".

Remember what we read earlier about Methuselah. His name means "when he dies, judgment". Basically, when Methuselah died, judgment came by the way of the flood. Judgment is when the light exposes those who have wicked works. The flood separated everyone into two groups. Those who were found guilty, engulfed by the flood and those who were not guilty, which was Noah and his family. The flood was not punishment. It was just a way to separate everyone into two groups. In fact, back in Noah's day, God never said man was evil. He simply said the wickedness **of** man was great in the earth. The wickedness **of** man is the actions and behavior coming out **of** the man, such as the deeds **of** man, but not man himself.

Then we see in **John 5:22-29 (ESV)**, it says v22 "For the Father judges no one, but has given all judgment to the Son, v23 that all may honor the Son, just as they honor the Father. Whoever does not honor the son does not honor the Father who sent him. v24 Truly, truly, I say to you, whoever hears my word and believes him who sent me has eternal life. He does not come into judgment but has passed from death to life. v25 "Truly, truly, I say to you, an hour is coming, and is now here, when the dead will hear the voice of the Son of God, and those who hear will live. v26 For as the Father has life in himself, so he has granted the Son also to have life in himself. v27 And, he has given him authority to execute judgment, because he is the Son of Man. v28 Do not marvel at this, for an hour is coming when all who are in the tombs will hear his voice v29 and come out, those who have done good to the resurrection of life, and those who have done evil to the resurrection of judgment".

Let's notice a few things:

1. The Father judges no one. All judgment is given to the son. This makes sense since Jesus, the son, is the light. It says in v27 He (The Father) has given Him (Jesus) authority to execute judgment and

expose the evil works of those on the team of unbelievers.

2. Those who believe Him (The Father) who sent Jesus has eternal life and **DOES NOT** come into judgment. They **do not** get exposed by the light. They pass directly from death to life since they embrace the light. Then those who don't embrace the light will stay where they are for now.

3. Since judgment in these verses is talking about exposing those who have done wicked deeds, this **DOES NOT** mean sentencing them to death. This is just the process of separating them from the team of believers. The guilty in one group and the not guilty in another group. It's like a drug raid where the police arrest everyone and sort it all out later. You had no idea! You were just hanging out, but you got arrested too. The evidence indicated that you are not guilty. You had nothing to do with it, so the judge lets you go. But everyone else was found guilty so they had to stay where they are.

4. Now we see that those who believe in Jesus will pass **DIRECTLY** from death to life. But what happens to those who are unbelievers. Death is off the table since Jesus already paid the price. So, what does happen to the unbeliever? Instead of passing

directly from death to life, the unbelievers take the long way from death to life. Remember Eternal Life is a free gift. They eventually make it to life, but not until they go through the wrath of God.

5. First, they are judged and identified as an unbeliever and grouped together with all the other unbelievers, all of those who are guilty. Then, this entire group, this entire team of unbelievers, goes through the wrath of God together.

6. Then continuing in v29 we see John talking about two different resurrections. One is the resurrection to life for the believers. Then a second resurrection which is a resurrection to judgment for the unbelievers, those who have evil deeds. Take a closer look for a minute. One group is resurrected to life, but the second group does **NOT** get resurrected to death, eternal destruction, or Hell. They are resurrected to judgment. Only because they are part of the group who has been identified as the evil doers.

7. They are **NOT** being punished or sentenced. God has two different roads, two different paths. One path is directly from death to life for the group of believers and the other path is for the unbeliever.

8. Also, notice this interesting fact back in v28: both the good and the evil doers are still in the grave. As mentioned earlier, no one has gone to Heaven or to Hell according to the Bible.

According to **II Corinthians 5:10 (ESV)** both the good and the evil must appear before the judgment seat of Jesus. It says, "For we must all appear before the judgment seat of Christ, so that each one may receive what is due for what he has done in the body, whether good or evil". Now, that sounds more like sentencing. First judgment is made of who does good and who does evil, then we are sentenced or given what is due us according to what we have done in the body. We saw above that the believers will pass directly from death to life. This is what is due them. However, it doesn't say what the sentencing or punishment is for the evil doers / unbelievers, except they are resurrected to judgment and the wrath of God remains on them.

Of course, we saw earlier that the wages of sin is death. So, would the evil doers be sentenced to death? We also read earlier that Jesus already paid the price for **ALL** sin and destroyed both sin and the penalty for sin. However, we still have all these people who died in the 4000 years before Jesus and all the unbelievers after Jesus who will be resurrected from the grave to the resurrection of judgment. So, what is their sentence? We don't know. The Bible doesn't explain that yet. But

JUDGMENT

death is off the table. That just leaves life and since the believers go **directly** from death to life, then the unbelievers must take the long way from death to life. Because the penalty of death is no longer valid after Jesus paid the price for **ALL** sin. They literally have no place to go. They can either stay where they are or turn around and confess Jesus. And they can't really stay where they are any longer, so that just leaves one option. Just like we read in the Bible earlier that eventually every knee will bow and every tongue confess.

Even Peter was wondering what happens to the unbeliever when he says in **I Peter 4:17-18 (ESV)**, v17 "For it is time for judgment to begin at the household of God; and if it begins with us, what will be the outcome for those who do not obey the gospel of God? v18 And, If the **righteous is scarcely saved**, what will become of the ungodly and the sinner?"

If it was obvious that sinners were all sentenced to death or Hell, then why was Peter confused? And why did he ask that question? However, he did understand that the **righteous are scarcely saved.** If God's plan was to destroy everyone else and only walk away with just a handful of believers, that sounds like a weak plan and Jesus' sacrifice was a huge waste of time. So, are you telling me that God, as powerful as He is, couldn't come up with a better plan than this? Actually, He did! God has a plan for all the unbelievers. That's why there are two resurrections. One resurrection directly to life and the other one to judgment.

Well, here is an interesting thought or question. Since the unbelievers / evil doers are part of the second resurrection and they will be resurrected to judgment, then why bring them back to life just to kill them again during sentencing? Why not just leave them in the grave and be done with it? It doesn't make sense, makes me wonder. As you can see, Peter wasn't sure about that either.

Once again, Peter is talking about judgment in **II Peter 2 (ESV)**. We read this earlier, but Peter is writing his words of encouragement and using some examples of the greatness of God where he says in v4 that if God did not spare the angels who sinned but committed them to chains of gloomy darkness and kept there until the judgment. Then, in v9, it says "then the Lord knows how to rescue the godly from trials, and to keep the unrighteous under punishment until the day of judgment.

As you can see here, there is a day, a future day of judgment when the light will come to separate the dark from the light, the good from the evil, the believer from the unbeliever. That day is NOT now, it's NOT when you die, but it will be coming soon. Also, you can see that the angels who sinned are kept in chains until the judgment. So, they will have to face judgment as well. They have not been sentenced either. They are kept in chains, in a holding cell here on earth, not in Hell, waiting for their court date.

Jude also talks about this in **Jude 1:6 (ESV)** where it says, "And the angels who did not stay within their own position of authority, but left their proper dwelling, he has kept in eternal chains under gloomy darkness until the judgment of the great day". Then Jude points out in v7, that when God destroyed Sodom and Gomorrah by fire it was an example of what will happen in the day of judgment. Read it in v7, "just as Sodom and Gomorrah and the surrounding cities, which likewise indulged in sexual immorality and pursued unnatural desire, serve as an example by undergoing a punishment of eternal fire".

Notice a couple of things. When the Bible uses the term: eternal chains or eternal fire, it does not literally mean forever. Or, when you hear the term: eternal torment, it does not always mean forever either. It's just an expression like when we say I **never** do that, or he is **always** like that. Never and always are just expressions and doesn't always mean literally. When Jude uses the expression eternal chains it was temporary, for a limited period of time, until the day of judgment. And, when Sodom and Gomorrah underwent punishment by eternal fire, we know the city burned down and eventually the fire went out, so it's obvious, in these cases, that eternal does not mean forever.

So far, we found out that judgment, according to **John 3:19 (ESV)** is when light enters the world to separate those who come to the light and those who have done wickedness and hide from the light. Basically, the light exposes those who are guilty. To demonstrate this, Jude references a prophecy from the day of Enoch in **Jude 1:14-16 (ESV)** where it says, v14 "It was also about these that Enoch, the seventh from Adam, prophesied, saying, "Behold, the Lord comes with ten thousands of his holy ones, v15 to execute judgment on all and to convict all the ungodly of all their deeds of ungodliness that they have committed in such an ungodly way, and of all the harsh things that ungodly sinners have spoken against him".

Here it says in v15 that the Lord will execute judgment on **ALL** (everyone) and to convict **ALL** the ungodly of their deeds of ungodliness. All the ungodly is a sub-group of all people. And, remember in John 5, it says the Father judges no one and all authority has been given over to the son to execute judgment. That makes sense since Jesus (The Son) is the Lord and the light. And it's the light that exposes those who have wicked deeds, the ungodly.

Upon whom does He execute judgment? In **Jude 1:15 (ESV)** it says on **ALL**, that's everyone. Then after He executes judgment on **ALL** people, He separates them into two groups by taking **ALL** the ungodly out of the group of **ALL** people and puts them in their own group. He does this by convicting them, the ungodly, of all their deeds of ungodliness. And, until now, **NO ONE** has been sentenced.

The main thing to remember is that judgement is the process of separating those who are guilty and those who are not guilty. Sentencing comes later. Although, we know, according to the Bible, that the wages of sin is death. Therefore, at this point, we might assume if we are found guilty, we will be sentenced to death. However, Jesus already paid the price / fulfilled the death sentence. So, what happens to those who are convicted / found guilty since Jesus already paid the price? They have no place to go, the price has already been paid. They are still waiting, since it appears that this day of judgment has not yet happened.

On one hand, we read that **ALL** will come to repentance, but then we read that the ungodly will be judged and found guilty. However, Jesus paid the price for ALL sin, so the ungodly, the unbeliever has no place to go. They can't go to Heaven, they're an unbeliever. They can't go to Hell; Jesus destroyed the works of the devil. So, what actually happens on the Day of Judgment? We read that the Lord will convict them of their evil ways on the Day of Judgment. Well, just like the Lord has convicted all the believers before they became believers, He will also convict all the unbelievers on the Day of Judgment.

So, if God convicted you when you were still an unbeliever and made you a believer, then isn't it possible that God will do the same thing for this group of unbelievers on the day of judgment. Since the unbeliever has no place to go, the only option left is for them to repent and become a believer. And since Jesus came to **save the world**, then He must have come with a plan to make that happen. Otherwise, if His plan doesn't work out, then He failed. We've also read in many scriptures that **ALL** will be saved, and **ALL** will come to repentance, and **EVERY** tongue will confess. And we've read that the mystery of His plan is to unite **ALL** things in heaven and earth. This is God's plan and **He never fails**!

REVELATION

So, before we get too knee deep into the Book of Revelation, we need to understand a couple of Biblical concepts from back in the day. First of all, God made man in His image, after the God kind. Then He told Adam and Eve to unite as husband and wife and create children and make a family. And as Adam and Eve were expanding the population and creating a family, God was re-creating Himself through man with all these newborn baby humans who look just like God, created in His image, after the God kind.

We see back in the Old Testament the custom of the firstborn son who gets special privileges referred to as a birthright. They receive a special inheritance. There seems to be a parallel between the firstborn son and the harvest of the first fruits.

Back then, it was an agricultural society. You had the first harvest, which were the crops that grew first and then a second harvest called the ingathering at the end of the year to gather up everything else. And the first group of crops would be called the first fruits. It was common, even required, to bring the best part of first fruits to the priests as a special offering.

You can see an example in **Exodus 23:14-19 (ESV)**, v14 "Three times in the year you shall keep a feast to me. v15 You shall keep the Feast of Unleavened Bread. As I commanded you, you shall eat unleavened bread for seven days at the appointed time in the month of Abib, for in it you came out of Egypt. None shall appear before me empty-handed. v16 You shall keep the Feast of Harvest, of the first fruits of your labor, of what you sow in the field. You shall keep the Feast of Ingathering at the end of the year when you gather in from the field the fruit of your labor. v17 Three times in the year shall all your males appear before the Lord God. v18 You shall not offer the blood of my sacrifice with anything leavened or let the fat of my feast remain until the morning. v19 The best of the first fruits of your ground you shall bring into the house of the Lord your God".

Notice in v15 it was required. It says, "**None** shall appear before me empty-handed". And then again in verse 19, that they are **required** to bring the best of the first fruits to the house of the Lord. Take note that this was not just any ordinary first fruits, but the **best** of the first fruits. Some translations say **First** of the First Fruits. Either way, the principle is the same. It's the best of the best.

This agricultural principal and offering of the first fruits represent God's plan of salvation. God does everything in order, as you can see throughout the Bible. God is a planner with a specific goal in mind. He is working in stages, everything, and everyone in a specific order. Two harvests, one of the first fruits and one for the rest of the crops. Two resurrections, one of the first fruits and one for everyone else. In other words, not everyone gets saved at the same time or in the same way. In Exodus 23, there are three different events throughout the year. The first event is the Feast of Unleavened Bread, then we have the Feast of Harvest, which represents the first resurrection where Jesus will Harvest all His people eagerly waiting for Him. Then the third event is the Feast of Ingathering. This is the rest of the crop of salvation, the second resurrection. Those resurrected to judgment. Still part of the crop of salvation. God does everything in order.

But Wait! There are two harvest and two resurrections, but in **Exodus 23:14-15, 17 (ESV)** it mentions three times a year, three events. The Feast of Unleavened Bread, then Feast of Harvest, and the Feast of the Ingathering. Since this agricultural process represents God's plan of salvation, the first crop to come up out of the ground would be Jesus, literally resurrected out of the ground, the **first** of the first fruits. Then after Christ would be those in Christ, the believers, the first fruits, those eagerly waiting. Then thirdly, everyone else, referred to as the ingathering or the rest of the crop. Still part of the crop of salvation.

Why does the Feast of Unleavened Bread represent Christ's resurrection? Well, in **1 Corinthians 5:6 (ESV)** Paul says "Your boasting is not good. Do you not know that a little leaven, leavens the whole lump? Paul is using the term leaven as an analogy for sin. Leaven is the same thing as yeast or baking powder, which causes bread and biscuits to expand and get puffed up. Just like sin causes us to get puffed up and full of ourselves. Just like Paul said, "Your boasting is not good". Therefore, since Jesus is absent of sin and He came to destroy sin, this Feast of Unleavened Bread is absent of leaven, which also represents the absence of sin.

You can see this principle of the first fruits and how God does everything in order explained in **I Corinthians 15:20-23 (ESV)**, where it says v20 "But in fact Christ has been raised from the dead, the first fruits of those who have fallen asleep. v21 For, as by a man came death, by a man has come also the resurrection of the dead. v22 For as in Adam all die, so also **in Christ shall all be made alive**. v23 But, **each in his own order**: Christ the first fruits, then at his coming those who belong to Christ".

Take note once again that in Adam all die but in Christ **ALL** shall be made alive. That's everyone, but also note, **each in his own order** as mentioned in verse 23. First Jesus, then at his coming, those who belong to Christ. What about everyone else? They get saved later. **Each in**

his own order. Remember it says **ALL** shall be made alive, just not all at the same time. Now, this is about as clear as any statement can be in the Bible. It is not confusing or taken out of context. It's not Randy's idea or interpretation, it says **ALL** shall be made alive. We've read that in other scriptures as well, but some people read this and **STILL** don't believe God. Once you understand that Hell does not exist and it is just a myth, then everything else about God starts to make sense. He came up with a plan to save the world and He won't stop until He finishes the job.

Christ is the first fruits of those of us who believe. Just as the firstborn gets the birthright, Christ also gets the birthright for being God's firstborn son, but not only is Christ the first of the first fruits, but we who believe in Christ are the first fruits of everyone else who will be saved. You can see that in **II Thessalonians 2:13 (ESV)** where it says, "But we ought always to give thanks to God for you, brothers beloved by the Lord, because **God chose you as the first fruits to be saved**, through sanctification by the Spirit and belief in the truth".

Notice that God chose us, we did not choose Him. He chose a small group of believers to be saved first as the First Fruits. By definition, the word "first" means there must be more to follow, the rest of the crop. The rest of the crop will be harvested later, which is referred to as the ingathering. You can't have a first group to be saved without a second group. Otherwise, it wouldn't be first.

It would just be those who are saved. But God was very clear when He said that the believers will be the **FIRST** to be saved.

Then we see in **James 1:18 (ESV)**, it says "Of his own will he brought us forth by the word of truth, that we should be a kind of first fruits of his creatures". Here James says **of God's own will**, nothing about our will or our choice. It's very clear, "**Of His own will**". Not only that, but He **made us** kind of a first fruits. Not by our choice, He made us.

Then as we get into the book of Revelation, we will also see in **Revelations 14:4 (ESV)**, where it says "It is these who have not defiled themselves with women, for they are virgins. It is these who follow the Lamb wherever he goes. These have been redeemed from mankind as **first fruits** for God and the Lamb"

Now that we see how God uses the principle of the harvest and compares it to the harvest of His children into His family, His Kingdom, we can keep that in mind as we move into the book of Revelation.

Another thing to keep in mind as we move into **Revelation (ESV)** is that God has a plan. He came up with the idea of man and the sacrifice of Jesus a long time before He ever created man. He is well organized, strategic, and He does everything in order. God already planned on the first group called the first fruits, getting saved first. Then, He also planned on the second group going through the wrath of God but saved later. This is

God's plan! He is not making this stuff up as He goes along. He does **NOT** keep changing His plans because we keep messing up or changing our minds. Everything was already decided.

We have seen throughout the Bible that God has been separating everyone into two groups. **Revelation** is no different. We will see the two harvests, which represent the two resurrections. One to life, where the first fruits go directly from death to life and then the second harvest, which represent the second resurrection, which is the resurrection to judgment.

God's plan, God's choice was to create humans weak, knowing they would mess up and then Jesus would come and save the world, every human that ever existed. What about our choice? What if we don't want to be saved? We don't get a choice! God already came up with His endgame. He decided how His plan was going to turn out long before we were created. Sure, we have free choice throughout our human existence, but we don't have the right to change God's plan.

Remember this is God's plan, God's choice. Does our free choices control God's free choice to stick to a plan? Every time someone changes their mind, does God keep re-arranging the chess board? Is God and Jesus keeping score by saying, "Nope, lost another one, wait a minute, here's three more, oh my bad, only two more", and so on throughout history.

Is God's plan about our free choice or is God's plan about **GOD** and His free choice. That choice, that decision He made when He came up with a plan a long time ago, before He even created man with free choice.

We saw that all humans have sinned and the wages of sin is death. And, since God demands justice and it's too late for humans to redeem themselves. Jesus said, "you know what, I'll do it, I'll take the hit for the team, I'll pay the price". And, as we read earlier, Jesus paid the price for everyone, the whole world. And we saw that Jesus paid the price for **ALL** sin.

As we move into **Revelation (ESV)**, it tells a story of how God's plan ends. These end-time events such as the day of judgment, the wrath of God, the lake of fire, even the mark of the beast was all planned out ahead of time and part of God's plan. Revelation is **NOT** a demonstration of how God plans on punishing everyone. It is God showing us how He is going to win. God will save everyone, including this second harvest. That is how great God is! He has a plan from the beginning to save everyone in spite of whether we reject Him or decide to worship Satan at the last minute. This is God's plan, God's free choice, planned out long before He even gave man free choice. Our bad choices will never get in the way or control God's free choice, God's plan to save everyone.

As we get started, I wanted to break down the Book of Revelation one chapter at a time. However, since Revelation is so long and full of details, boring details, I decided to do an abbreviated version and just focus on the main point in each chapter.

So, here we go...let's dig into **Revelation 1:1 (ESV)**, where it says "The revelation of Jesus Christ, which God gave him to show to his servants the things that must soon take place. He made it known by sending his angel to his servant John".

Here we have the revelation of Jesus Christ about to be revealed by His angel, His messenger to John in a vision quest. The images and descriptions you'll see and read about are bizarre and strange. John doesn't really understand what he's seeing, but he writes everything down the best he can. Why did God pick John to do this? I don't know, but it does seem like John is more detailed in his writing than the other gospel writers: Matthew, Mark, & Luke.

As you start to read Revelation, you will notice it is very symbolic. John's vision is very much like a dream. You will see a lot of symbols and images that don't make any sense. Somehow, they represent the end-time events, but you cannot take them literally. They are only a vision, a sign of things to come, **NOT literal** things to come. It's like driving down the road and seeing a sign that says McDonald's up ahead with an image of Ronald McDonald eating a juicy hamburger. But, when you get there, you don't see Ronald McDonald and the hamburger, well, not so juicy. It was just a **sign** of things to come, not literally Ronald McDonald eating a hamburger.

In fact, the literal translation of **Revelation 1:1**, says "he did **signify**, having sent through his messenger to his servant John". What does "He did signify" mean? In other words, He sent a sign, a symbol, a billboard of things to come, through His angel the messenger. If we look up the direct translation from Greek to English it says, "He showed by signs". And other translations actually say these are a sign of things to come. These are not literal end-time events; however, they do represent the end-time events.

And, just to be clear, I am **NOT** going to try to interpret what these signs and symbols mean. But, if the Angel tells John and John tells us what some of these images mean that's fine, but the rest of the images remain a mystery. I might throw out a comment or two, but that's just me thinking out loud.

So, first we see John writing letters to the seven churches around Asia. John is chillin' on the island of Patmos getting some much-needed rest and relaxation on the Sabbath day, when all of a sudden, he hears a very loud voice, like a trumpet, behind him, interrupting his thought process as he's writing these letters. This voice he hears is telling him what to write to these seven churches. And it's telling him to write down what he sees and then send the letters to the churches. Then, John turns around and he sees this image of an angel. At first, he thought it was Jesus, but then again, he's probably thinking "What the …". And, as he sees this image, this angel, it was standing in the middle of seven lamp stands.

But this image was not Jesus. So, whoever it was, he had seven stars in his right hand and a two-edged sword coming out of his mouth. How Bizarre!

Then, in v17-19, John says "When I saw him, I fell at his feet as though dead. But he laid his right hand on me, saying, "Fear not, I am the first and the last", v18 and the living one. I died, and behold I am alive forevermore, and I have the keys of Death and Hades. v19 Write therefore the things that you have seen, those that are and those that are to take place after this".

This sounds like it's Jesus, the living one, the first and last, the one who died and is alive, etc., but we know from earlier in this chapter this had to be a messenger, speaking on behalf of Jesus...not literally Jesus.

But wait a minute! If this image had seven stars in his right hand, what happened to those seven stars when he placed his right hand upon John? Almost immediately we are seeing a lot of symbolism and images that **CANNOT** be taken literally.

Also, notice that this messenger, on behalf of Jesus, says he has the keys of death and hades. Keys represent control. He has control over death and hades. Not the messenger, but Jesus has control over death and hades. Remember earlier, Jesus destroyed death and hades. What about hades? Well hades is a Greek word that means the grave or abode of the dead. Whereas the translators used the word "Hell" to describe hades, which is the grave.

As for the seven stars John saw in the right hand of this mysterious stranger, it is clear that these images are not meant to be literal as this stranger, this messenger of Jesus explains in v20 "As for the mystery of the seven stars that you saw in my right hand, and the seven golden lampstands, the seven stars are the angels of the seven churches, and the seven lampstands are the seven churches".

Well, there you have it! The seven lampstands represent the churches, and the seven stars represent the angels of those churches. Then, this messenger, this angel, representing Jesus, tells John to finish writing his letters to the seven churches in Asia. But instead of writing them to the churches, he tells him to write them or address them to these seven angels of the churches, represented by the seven stars. Then, he tells him what to write. This you can see throughout all of **Revelation 2 and 3 (ESV)**.

Revelation 4 (ESV) –
- John gets swept up into Heaven, in the spirit. Is he having an out of body experience or is he having a dream? Either way...
- John sees a throne and twenty-four other thrones surrounding that throne.
- Then, in front of the throne he saw seven torches of fire burning.

- These seven torches were symbolic. They represented the seven spirits of God.
- Then John saw four bizarre creatures who talked. They were full of eyes and each one had six wings.

NOTE:

1. *What John was seeing were symbolic images. They are not meant to be taken literally. For instance, you see the seven torches represent the seven spirits of God. And the bizarre creatures were "like" a lion or "like" an ox, etc. They were like the creature, but they weren't the actual creature, they are symbolic of the something else.*

2. *The number twelve is used throughout the Bible to represent perfection. Twelve tribes of Israel, for instance. Twenty-Four elders (two groups of twelve) here in **Revelation 4 (ESV)**, etc.*

3. *The number seven is used throughout the Bible to represent completion. For instance, God rested on the seventh day of creation to represent He was done, it was complete.*

Revelation 5 (ESV) –
- Then John saw the image on the throne (from Chapter 4) holding a scroll in His right hand. Sealed with seven seals.
- No one was worthy to open it.
- John saw a lamb that "looked" like it was slain.
- Apparently this slain lamb was the only one worthy or else He wouldn't have grabbed it.
- Then John said in **Revelation 5:13 (ESV)** that he heard **EVERY** creature in heaven and on earth and under the earth and in the sea, and all that is in them, saying,

"To him who sits on the throne and to the Lamb be blessing and honor and glory and might forever and ever!"

NOTE:

1. *Here we see a lot of symbolism. Sometimes the messenger reveals the meaning to John, and he writes it down, but sometimes the meaning of the symbolism is not revealed.*

2. *We also see the number seven again in connection with the seven seals on the scroll.*

3. *Notice something very important. John heard **every** creature, that's **ALL** creatures in heaven, on earth, including **ALL** human creatures and creatures under the earth as well as creatures in the sea praising Him and giving glory to Him. Just like we saw earlier in the Bible where it said every tongue will confess the name of Jesus and every knee will bow. Every creature means everyone.*

Revelation 6 – 9 (ESV) –
- Here we see the Lamb opening the seven seals and then seven angels ready to blow seven trumpets.

Revelation 10 (ESV) –
- John saw another angel coming down from heaven. This angel was a mighty angel, and he was carrying a scroll. Kind of like the previous scroll, but this time it was a little scroll.
- Then, after all the trumpets, John saw the mighty angel raise his right hand and swear by God that there would be no more delay. That, in the day of the Trumpet call sounded by the seventh angel, the mystery of God would be fulfilled. What does he mean fulfilled? And what is this mystery? Basically, the mystery of God will be done, finished, complete. So, what mystery is he talking about?

NOTE:

1. *Remember **Ephesians 1:9-10 (ESV)** we discussed earlier? This is where Paul mentioned that God made known to us the **mystery of His will**, according to His purpose, which He set forth in Christ. And that plan in v10 was for the fullness of time, **to unite all things in Him**, things in heaven and things on earth. So, at the time of the seventh trumpet it must be the fullness of time and the mystery will be fulfilled. That same mystery mentioned in Ephesians, which is to unite **ALL** things in Him. **ALL** things in heaven and in earth. **That's everything and everybody**.*

2. *Not to mention, we just read in* **Revelation 5:13 (ESV)** *that* **EVERY** *creature would praise His name.*

Revelation 11 (ESV) –
- We see John writing about the two witnesses and a future event. Remember, this is all symbolic. For all we know, these two witnesses could be CNN & Fox News.

NOTE:

1. *Then in **Chapter 11:15**, we finally get to the seventh angel blowing the trumpet. Remember, from what we read earlier, this is when the mystery of God is*

*fulfilled. Earlier we read that the mystery of God is to unite **ALL** things in Him.*

2. *Angel 7 Trumpet – As the seventh angel blew his trumpet, there were loud voices in heaven, saying, "The kingdom of the world has become the kingdom of our Lord and of his Christ, and he shall reign forever and ever." The twenty-four elders worshiped God, saying:*

> *'We give thanks to you, Lord God Almighty, who is and who was, for you have taken your great power and begun to reign. The nations raged, but your wrath came, and the time for the dead to be judged, and for rewarding your servants, the prophets and saints, and those who fear your name, both small and great, and for destroying the destroyers of the earth'."*

Revelation 12 (ESV) –

- John sees more symbolic images. And we read about the event where Satan and his demons were kicked out of Heaven and thrown down to earth.

Revelation 13 (ESV) –

- John describes a beast coming out of the water. The more into Revelation we read, the more obvious that these images and events are all symbolic. And right now, these images are sounding like war time events.

NOTE:

1. *Whatever this beast is, we see it having authority for three and a half years. It is cussing God and those who dwell in Heaven. And those on the earth will be worshipping it. It says in v8, "and all who dwell on earth will worship it, everyone whose name has not been written **before the foundation of the world in the book of life** of the Lamb who was slain".*

2. *This tells me that everyone on the earth at that time are also those whose name is not written **before the foundation of the world in the book of life.** So, where is everyone else, the ones that are saved, those on the team of believers?*

3. *What does he mean "before the foundation of the world"? We've heard that expression before... Well, remember what Paul said in **Ephesians 1:3-4 (ESV)**, v3 "Blessed be the God and Father of our Lord Jesus Christ, who has blessed us in Christ with every spiritual blessing in the heavenly places, v4 even as **He chose us in him before the foundation***

***of the world**, that we should be holy and blameless before Him. In love".*

4. *So, whatever this book of life is, it was written before the foundation of the world. God chose us before the foundation of the world, and we read earlier we were saved before the ages began. All before God started with creation. He already added your name to the book of life long before you were born. God has been working since the beginning of time so you can be born at the proper time. God is in charge, and He has a plan. He has to be intricately involved in every detail in order for His plan to work. God will not let our free choice interfere or get in the way of His plan.*

5. *Not only did He write your name in the book of life **before the foundation of the world**, but everyone whose name was **NOT** written in the book of life was left out intentionally **before the foundation of the world**. And now, in **Chapter 13**, they are all left on earth worshiping the beast.*

6. *Also, remember what Peter said in **I Peter 1 (ESV)**, "**Jesus was slain before the foundation of the world**". This entire plan of God, including Jesus getting crucified, whose names are in the book*

of life, and who's not in the book of life was well planned out in advance.

7. *Then continuing with John's vision, he saw a second beast. The second beast **causes** (forces) everyone to receive the mark of the beast. It says in **Revelation 13:16-17 (ESV)**, "it **causes all**, both small and great, both rich and poor, both free and slave, to be marked on the right hand or the forehead, v17 so that no one can buy or sell unless he has the mark."*

8. *Wow! Let's read that again. Everyone on earth **WILL** be worshiping the first beast and the second beast causes **ALL** (everyone) to be marked with the mark of the beast. Now that is interesting!! I was always taught that when the time comes, some will "**choose**" the mark of the beast and they will be lost forever, but if you just have faith and refuse the mark you will be saved. However, that is simply **NOT** true! You **DO NOT** get a choice!*

As you can see, **Revelation** is full of symbolism, signs, images, mysterious creatures, and strange events with vague descriptions, that are soon to come. It doesn't matter if you have a doctorate in theology or you're the smartest person in the world, unless **Revelation** explains itself, there is no way to figure out what all this means. Anything you come up with is only speculation. The rest of the Bible is very clear, easy to understand, but when it comes to **Revelation** it's just a dream, a vision given to John. He does his best to describe what he sees, but we may never understand what it all means. Possibly when these events occur, we might be able to put two and two together and see some similarities, but then again maybe not.

Basically, all I'm doing here is summarizing John's vision as he describes each event in his dream. Then if something seems to make sense or **Revelation** explains some of the symbols, I'll add some commentary. In the meantime, let's move on to **Chapter 14**.

However, before we just jump right in, we have to look back at **Chapter 13** for a minute, because these two chapters actually go together. First, we read in **Chapter 13** that **everyone** on the earth would be worshiping the first beast and the second beast would cause or force **ALL** (everyone) to receive the mark of the beast. They don't get a choice. This is part of God's plan. He's just explaining the sequence of events of what's going to happen. So where are these two groups, these two teams we keep hearing about? Where is the team of believers, those who are saved when we see everyone on earth worshipping the beast? And, where does the Bible say that God's people will be required to make a choice and refuse the mark of the beast?

If we move onto **Chapter 14**, we can answer some of those questions...

Revelation 14 (ESV) –

- Here we see 144,000 getting sealed on their foreheads by Jesus' name and by His Father's name. In v4 it says, "These have been redeemed from mankind as **firstfruits** for God and the Lamb".

NOTE:

1. *Here are the two groups! We see God doing it again...separating everyone. Those with Jesus' name on their foreheads and everyone else with the mark of the beast on their foreheads.*

   *Whereas those with Jesus' name have already been redeemed from mankind, so they are no longer part of the group that God is referring to when He says **everyone on the earth** would be worshiping the beast. They are already redeemed and marked with the name of Jesus.*

2. *Remember we read earlier about the **first fruits**. Those redeemed from mankind were redeemed as **first fruits**. Everyone is in one of the two groups. You are either grouped with the **first fruits** or you are part of the rest of the crop. Whenever you have a first, it implies more to come...at least a second one will follow.*

3. *So, here it is, what we read earlier...*

4. ***II Thessalonians 2:13 (ESV)****, it says "But we ought always to give thanks to God for you, brothers beloved by the Lord, because **God chose you as the first fruits to be saved**, through sanctification by the Spirit and belief in the truth".*

5. *Then again in **James 1:18 (ESV)**, it says "Of his own will he brought us forth by the word of truth, that we should be a kind of first fruits of his creatures".*

Here I want to elaborate on Angel 3 in **Chapter 14** where John saw three angels, each with a message, whereas Angel 3 says:

Angel 3 – "If anyone worships the beast and its image and receives a mark on his forehead or on his hand, he also will drink the wine of God's wrath, poured full strength into the cup of his anger, and he will be tormented with fire and sulfur in the presence of the holy angels and in the presence of the Lamb. And the smoke of their torment goes up forever and ever, and they have no rest, day or night, these worshipers of the beast and its image, and whoever receives the mark of its name".

Here again, God is explaining the sequence of events that was already decided from the beginning as part of His plan. So, don't misunderstand this Angel. This is not some kind eternal existence in Hell. We've already established that Hell is an old English word that means to cover or conceal. And we've seen that Satan has been rendered powerless. Besides Jesus destroyed the works of the devil, including sin and death.

Angel 3 is talking about all those who are still on earth, those who have not been redeemed. Those who have not been saved. They were worshiping the beast and they all have the mark of the beast. They are part of the "other" group. So, what happens to them? Angel 3 is saying that they will...

1. **Drink the wine of God's wrath**
2. **Be tormented (not tortured) with fire and sulfur**
3. **They will have no rest.**

That's it! That's all that happens to them. This was all part of God's plan from the beginning, before He even created man, before man sinned. God had a plan! Man's free choice to make bad choices does not **FORCE** God to change His plans. He did not just come up with this idea because man sinned. If that was the case, then God's actions, God's rules, God's plan would be completely dictated by man's choices. That would make the creation greater than the creator. But instead, God's plan **WILL** happen in spite of man's choices.

Besides, this is not some kind of punishment. There is no mention of Hell or a fiery pit for eternity. And there is no mention of sins. Jesus already paid the price for all sin. The angel is only explaining the rules. Just like John mentioned in **John 3:16 (ESV)** that those who believe will not perish. They will move to the front of the line. Whereas here we have the angel explaining what happens to the other team. The team of unbelievers.

So, what does all this mean? I'm not sure, but what I am sure about is that it doesn't say anything about Hell or punishment. And it is reasonable to conclude that these events are symbolic since everything else in Revelation is symbolic. You can't take this literally. Tormented with fire and sulfur is not literally fire and sulfur.

And, when the Angel says the smoke of their torment goes up forever, it doesn't say anything about being tormented forever. Just the **smoke** of their torment would go up forever. Also, the word torment has been used in the Bible several times to mean regret. Basically, that's just an expression.

Not to mention, John explains in v12 that Angel 3 was only saying these things to encourage the saints to endure. It was a reminder of the benefits of being part of the first team, the first fruits, the team of believers. We will go directly from death to life, while avoiding (saved from) these end-time events.

Now we are starting to get to the meat of **Revelation**, which is exciting, but it also means I'm going to elaborate more. It will get a bit wordy, but I will be summarizing as much as I can.

Now, continuing in **Revelation 14 (ESV),** John sees a white cloud and seated on the cloud one like a son of man, with a golden crown on his head, and a sharp sickle in his hand.

Notice the symbolism!

A sickle is a tool used for harvesting. Here again we have an analogy comparing a physical harvest to a spiritual harvest of God's people. We also see a white cloud. White has been used to represent clean and pure in the Bible. And then we see the image on the white cloud, which looks "**LIKE**" a son of man, referring to Jesus. John's dream is a picture of what will take place in the future, but it was not the actual event. It was a "picture" of the event.

Then, as John continues to dream or have this vision, he saw another angel coming out of the temple, calling out to the image on the cloud, and saying "Put in your sickle, and reap, for the hour to reap has come, for the harvest of the earth is fully ripe." Then John saw the image on the white cloud swing His sickle and the earth was reaped. Harvest the earth of what? What are the crops? Well, it's reasonable to conclude, since God compares a physical harvest to a spiritual harvest, that this is referring to the time that Jesus rescues the first fruits, those who believe, those who are saved.

Then as we continue some more, John sees two more angels. One coming out of the temple in heaven, who had a sharp sickle as well. And the other one came out from the altar, who has authority over the fire, and this one called out to the other one with the sharp sickle and said in v18, "Put in your sickle and gather the clusters from the vine of the earth, for its grapes are ripe". So, the angel swung his sickle across the earth and gathered the grape harvest of the earth and threw it into the great winepress of the wrath of God.

Here we see a second harvest. The rest of the crop, the rest of the people left on earth, who we saw worshiping the beast, those with the mark of the beast, the unbeliever. It looks like this second harvest is ripe and ready to go. Then, once it's harvested, it gets thrown into the great winepress of the wrath of God. What in the world is the great winepress of the wrath of God?

Well, think about the symbolism of the harvest for a minute. Here we have two separate harvests. First you have the image on the white horse and the image on the horse was reaping the earth, which is the first harvest, first fruits, those who believed. Then another harvest was reaped, a second harvest, which were grapes that were ripe. These grapes were ready to be harvested, but yet they were thrown into the great winepress of the **wrath of God**. They were ripe, but not yet finished. They still needed to go through another process before they were ready.

Typically, we think about this second group, the second harvest as those going to Hell or punished for sin, especially for rejecting Jesus. But the Bible never says that. In fact, we just read that the second harvest will get thrown into the great winepress of the **wrath of God**.

Think about a winepress for a minute. A winepress puts pressure on the grapes and churns up the grapes until they are perfect for producing wine. Typically, we identify the wrath of God as being something bad or something to avoid, but in this case the wrath of God is depicted as a great winepress, which is used for refining the grapes.

As we saw earlier, sometimes when we hear the word wrath or anger, we think of our human reactions of yelling, losing our temper, throwing things getting fed up, etc., but these are all human reactions. But God's wrath is compared to a winepress.

Calming behavior, taking action to make a positive change, helping someone who has hurt you, making rational decisions are **ALL** reactions to anger as well. So, when you encounter the wrath of God, it is not pleasant, but it is out of love when God is making a positive change in your life. And in the case of the great winepress of the wrath of God; it is where God is refining the grapes to perfection.

Revelation 15 (ESV) –
- John saw seven angels in Heaven with seven plagues. He said in v1 "Then I saw another sign in heaven, great and amazing, seven angels with seven plagues, which are the last, for with them the wrath of God is finished". This is very clear. John was seeing, once again, **a sign in Heaven**, a billboard, or a symbol of some kind.

NOTE:

1. Here we are in the middle of the event referred to as the wrath of God when John sees another sign in Heaven.

2. These seven angels, these seven plagues are the last. The event is almost over and with the seven angels the event called the wrath of God will be done.

Then those who had conquered the beast and its image, and the number of its name started singing. These are the first fruits, those who believed, those who are already redeemed, those who are saved. It was only those who conquered the beast who sang this song of Moses, the song of the lamb, which goes like this...

"Great and amazing are your deeds, O Lord God the Almighty! Just and true are your

> *ways, O King of the nations! Who will not fear, O Lord, and glorify your name? For you alone are holy. All nations will come and worship you, for your righteous acts have been revealed."*

Listen to their song very closely. They understood by their song, that **ALL** nations will worship Him. Here we have God's saints, those who conquered the beast, those who have already been redeemed and saved. They are excited to be singing this song.

If this group of saints, those who are saved are the only ones to make it and everyone else is lost, then why are they singing **ALL** nations **WILL** come and worship Him? They are singing **WILL** come, referring to a future event.

Also, in this song, they ask this rhetorical question, "Who will not fear, O Lord, and glorify your name?". They understood that it didn't make any sense that anyone would **NOT** fear Him or glorify His name.

Revelation 16 (ESV) –
- John heard a voice from the temple telling the seven angels to pour out on the earth the seven bowls of the wrath of God. All of these things are images and visions...signs and billboards of things to come, but not literal things to come. I'm not trying to interpret all this but show you

the symbolism of it all. There is nothing literal about **Revelation**, although it does represent real events, but the images are all symbolic.

After all this craziness, it's time to move into **Chapter 17**...

Revelation 17 (ESV) –
- John was visited by one of the seven angels who had the seven bowls. The angel wanted to show him the judgment of the great prostitute. Immediately, it's obvious this is not actually a physical person. This is an analogy or symbolic of something. Remember earlier, we saw that the judgment is when the light shines and exposes those who do evil deeds. In other words, the group of unbelievers.

NOTE:

1. When John saw her, he marveled greatly. But the angel asked him, why do you marvel. And he told John that he would tell him the mystery of the woman, and of the beast with seven heads and ten horns that carries her. The angel explained that the beast he saw, was, and is not, and is about to rise from the bottomless pit and go to destruction. And the **dwellers on earth whose names have not been written in the book of life from the foundation of**

the world will marvel to see the beast, because it was and is not and is to come.

2. Then the angel explained that the seven heads are seven mountains on which the woman is seated; they are also seven kings, five of whom have fallen, one is, the other has not yet come, and when he does come, he must remain only a little while. As for the beast that was and is not, it is an eighth, but it belongs to the seven, and it goes to destruction. And the ten horns that you saw are ten kings who have not yet received royal power, but they are to receive authority as kings for one hour, together with the beast. These are of one mind, and they hand over their power and authority to the beast. They will make war on the Lamb, and the Lamb will conquer them, for He is Lord of lords and King of kings, and those with him are called and chosen and faithful.

That is great! The angel explains everything and tells us what some of these symbols mean. Although, after hearing that explanation, I think I'm **more confused than I was before**. However, it is reasonable to conclude that the beast rising from the bottomless pit could be Satan, since he was thrown into the bottomless pit and locked away for 1,000 years as we read earlier. So, it sounds like this is the time after the 1,000 years and Satan gets released. Another thing I know is that this is a bunch of symbolism. Of course, we've seen earlier that the Lamb represents Jesus, and He kicks some ass.

Then the Angel explained that the waters that the prostitute sat represented people, nations, and languages. And the ten horns mentioned earlier, represent the ten kings not in power yet and the beast will hate the prostitute. They will make her desolate and naked and devour her flesh and burn her up with fire for **God has put it into their hearts to carry out His purpose by being of one mind and handing over their royal power to the beast, until the words of God are fulfilled**.

Notice that **God himself puts into the hearts** of the ten kings to make the prostitute desolate and naked and burn her up with fire. It was all God's doing. These ten kings did not get a choice. **God put it into their hearts to carry out HIS purpose**. Are you hearing that? It's God who is doing all this! It's all part of His plan, **HIS** purpose. God has a game plan, and we are the game pieces.

Revelation 18 (ESV) –
- John saw another angel with great authority making an announcement that the great city of Babylon has fallen. Then, continuing to announce with a loud voice that this great city of Babylon has become a dwelling place for demons.

Revelation 19 (ESV) –
- John heard rejoicing in Heaven. What sounded to him like a crowd of angels saying:

> *"Hallelujah! Salvation and glory and power belong to our God, for his judgments (Exposure of the evil doers) are true and just; for he has judged the great prostitute who corrupted the earth with her immorality and has avenged on her the blood of his servants".*
>
> *They yelled out again and said "Hallelujah! The smoke from her goes up forever and ever."*

And the twenty-four elders and the four living creatures fell down and worshiped God who was seated on the throne, saying, "Amen. Hallelujah!" And from the throne came a voice saying, "Praise our God, all you his servants, you who fear him, small and great".

Then John thought he heard another crowd of angels saying:

> *"Hallelujah! For the Lord our God the Almighty reigns. Let us rejoice and exult and give him the glory, for the marriage of*

the Lamb has come, and his Bride has made herself ready; it was granted her to clothe herself with fine linen, bright and pure for the fine linen is the righteous deeds of the saints".

This is where the saints, the first fruits symbolically marry the lamb dressed in fine linen, bright, and pure.

Then the angels said to John, "Write this: Blessed are those who are invited to the marriage supper of the Lamb. **These are the true words of God.**" In other words, everything else John saw was symbolism, but these are the **true** words of God.

Now we are getting to the good part in v11 when John saw heaven opened, and behold, John saw a white horse! The one sitting on it is called Faithful and True, and in righteousness he judges and makes war. His eyes are like a flame of fire, and on his head are many diadems, and he has a name written that no one knows but himself. He is clothed in a robe dipped in blood, and the name by which he is called is The Word of God. And the armies of heaven, arrayed in fine linen, white and pure, were following him on white horses. From his mouth comes a sharp sword with which to strike down the nations, and he will rule them with a rod of iron. He will tread the winepress of the fury of the wrath of God the Almighty. On his robe and on his thigh, he has a name written, King of kings and Lord of lords.

Remember, in **Chapter 14** we saw the crop of grapes harvested. They were ripe and ready to be harvested, but then thrown into the winepress. Keep in mind, this is the same analogy. In the process of making wine, the winepress is necessary to finish the process. God is not done with them yet!

Then John is seeing some more bizarre images about an end time war. He sees the beast and his army getting ready to make war against Him who sits on the white horse and His army. This image of Him who sits on the white horse is easy to figure out that it's talking about Jesus, since white represents clean and pure. A lot of the other symbols and images in **Revelation** are not that obvious.

Now, once that's all said and done and the battle is over, John saw that the beast was captured, and with it was the false prophet. The false prophet was the one who did all the signs that deceived those who received the mark of the beast and those who worshiped the beast's image. Then John saw both the beast and the false prophet thrown alive into the lake of fire. And the rest of the army was slain by the sword that came from the mouth of Him who was sitting on the horse. So, what is the lake of fire? This is the first time we're hearing about it. Although, in Matthew, we read about the eternal fire prepared for the devil and his angels. That could be the same fire, but it was only mentioned once or twice before Revelation. However, this is **NOT** a literal lake of fire. It's all part of John's vision and the images he saw. Symbolic of something, just like everything else.

A lot of people think the lake of fire represents Hell, but earlier we learned that Hell was hardly mentioned and mostly by Jesus when He was referencing the Valley of Gehenna, never about a fiery pit where sinners go. Then I question why the Valley of Gehenna was translated as Hell, when it was obviously **NOT** Hell, but the lake of fire was **NOT** translated as Hell at all. Yet a lot of people assume it is Hell, but that's just an assumption.

Moving on to **Chapter 20**, things get very interesting...

Revelations 20 (ESV) –
- Here John sees an angel with a key to the bottomless pit. He grabs Satan and throws his ass in there and locks him up for a thousand years, so he can't deceive anyone for a thousand years. After the thousand years, he'll be released for a little while. This is the same thousand years mentioned earlier.

Then what happens during the thousand years of peace? Well, John saw souls (creatures) that were killed for their belief in Jesus and those who did not worship the beast or partake in the mark of the beast. Keep in mind, these believers never went to Heaven, they were still dead... in the grave. However, once Satan was locked up, that's when John saw all these believers come back to life. We are talking Noah, David, Moses, Abraham, and the rest of the crew, all the believers throughout history. Then what did they do once they came back to life? They reigned with Christ for a thousand years. So, the timeline goes like this: According to Revelation, Satan is locked up and then the team of believers goes up to be with Jesus, not when they die. They are still in the grave **waiting** to be resurrected. Just like we saw in the Old Testament where the Hebrew word Sheol was used to describe the abode of the dead, whereas the word abode means a **waiting** place. Waiting to be resurrected.

As mentioned earlier, this is the first harvest, the first resurrection. Everyone else is still dead in the grave, not in Hell as some might think. Besides, Satan is locked up and otherwise detained at the moment. He can't really do anything about it right now anyway. All of the unbelievers, the rest of the dead, will be brought back to life in a second resurrection, after the thousand years. Just like we read earlier. There is a resurrection to life and 1,000 years later there will be a resurrection to judgment, which would be the second harvest, also called the harvest of the ingathering. Now the pieces are starting to fit together.

We can also see this resurrection to judgment in **Hebrews 9:27 (ESV)** where it says "it is appointed for man to die once, and after that comes judgment. It does **NOT** say after that comes Hell or death; it says judgment.

In the meantime, read **Revelation 20:1-6 (ESV)** for yourself, "Then I saw an angel coming down from heaven, holding in his hand the key to the bottomless pit and a great chain. v2 And, he seized the dragon, that ancient serpent, who is the devil and Satan, and bound him for a thousand years, v3 and threw him into the pit, and shut it and sealed it over him, so that he might not deceive the nations any longer, until the thousand years were ended. After that he must be released for a little while".

v4 "Then I saw thrones and seated on them were those to whom the authority to judge was committed. Also, I saw the souls of those who had been beheaded for the testimony of Jesus and for the word of God, and those who had not worshiped the beast or its image and had not received its mark on their foreheads or their hands. They came to life and reigned with Christ for a thousand years. v5 The rest of the dead did not come to life until the thousand years were ended. This is the first resurrection. v6 Blessed and holy is the one who shares in the first resurrection! Over such the **second death** has no power, but they will be priests of God and of Christ, and they will reign with him for a thousand years".

Remember earlier we saw that the believers would pass directly from death to life. That's what the first resurrection is all about. What in the world is the "**second death**" mentioned in v6? And what is meant by the second death has no power? We'll take a look at that in a little bit.

Not only will the believers, the faithful who are dead **in the grave**, who died in Christ, be resurrected to everlasting life, but those believers still alive will be changed into their new spiritual bodies, all part of the first resurrection. First, God resurrects those who already died in Christ and Jesus will bring them with him when He returns. Then as He's returning, those still alive will be changed to spirit and meet them in the clouds, Christ and those who were resurrected.

You can see Paul talking about that in **I Thessalonians 4:13-17 (ESV)** where it says, v13 "But we do not want you to be uninformed, brothers, about those who are asleep, that you may not grieve as others do who have no hope. v14 For, since we believe that Jesus died and rose again, even so, through Jesus, God will bring with him those who have fallen asleep. v15 For, this we declare to you by a word from the Lord, that we who are alive, who are left until the coming of the Lord, will not precede those who have fallen asleep. v16 For the Lord himself will descend from heaven with a cry of command, with the voice of an archangel, and with the sound of the trumpet of God. And the dead in Christ will rise first. v17 Then we who are alive, who are left, will be caught up together with them in the clouds to meet the Lord in the air, and so we will always be with the Lord".

Remember we read earlier, when Jesus returns, He is **NOT** dealing with sin. He is only bringing salvation to the group of believers. That still leaves all the unbelievers with nowhere to go. They are still in the grave waiting.

Basically, we see...

1. The angel locking Satan up for 1,000 years.

2. Then, the first thing that happens is the dead in Christ are resurrected to spiritual life.

3. Next, Jesus comes back, bringing these newly resurrected spirits with Him.

4. Then after that, the believers, still alive, will change to their new spirit forms and meet Jesus in the clouds with all the newly resurrected spirits.

5. Then, they will all reign with Christ for 1,000 years. Who are they going to reign over? I'm assuming all the other humans who are still alive, the unbelievers, living their existence. However, they are living in peace without the pressures of Satan since he is locked up. Besides, everyone else, all the unbelievers, who have died, are still in the grave, not Hell as some might think. It says right there in **Revelation 20:5 (ESV)**, "The rest of the dead **did not come to life** until the thousand years were ended". God has a plan, and He does everything in order.

Some believe that we have this lifetime and this lifetime only to decide if we want to accept or reject Jesus. If that was the case, then why didn't God just shut everything down after the first resurrection. God already had His people, His believers. Everyone else made their choice, right? However, these new saints, those resurrected first will reign with Christ for 1,000 years. Why? Seems like a waste of time if everyone else is lost anyway.

Remember God has a plan. And His plan, from the beginning, was a winning plan. He would resurrect the believers first, then His plan included a way to cleanse and purify everyone else who didn't believe Him at first. In order to do this, God included a second resurrection, all planned out from the beginning, as part of His winning plan.

Think about that again logically. According to common belief, once God resurrects his believers, everyone else is destroyed and thrown into Hell or the lake of fire. God is done, He has his people, His believers. Although, God did not do so good, His plan did not work out as well as He intended. He lost a lot more than He expected. If that was true, then why are the saints, the believers ruling with Christ while humans are still living their lives and reproducing more humans for another 1,000 years. Something isn't adding up. God is not done! He has a plan to save everyone else too. **God does not lose!**

After the thousand years. Satan was released from prison, and he was pissed! He gathered up his army, got the band back together and surrounded the saints and as he was getting ready to pounce, then fire came down from Heaven and consumed him. Then, he was thrown into the lake of fire. Now we are hearing about the lake of fire a second time. So far, we have the beast, the false prophet and now Satan in the lake of fire. Looks like God is gathering together all the "bad actors" in one place. Remember, this is not a literal lake of fire. This is an image John is seeing in his dream, his vision quest. He is writing things down and describing the images the best he can as he sees them.

We know who Satan is and the false prophet sounds like he could be an evangelist gone bad, who's been given false powers to create signs to deceive people, but who or what is this beast. This beast was mentioned multiple times, but who is he? According to **Revelation,** it appears to be something or somebody in which ten world leaders felt comfortable enough to turn over their authority. In other words, a superpower. To John, he sees a beast, a wild animal. Could that be symbolic of this superpower acting like a wild animal. We can't really say, we won't know until it happens. Then it will make more sense.

Now we finally get to the Day of Judgment! After the thousand years are up, after Satan gets thrown into the lake of fire, then John sees a bunch of dead people and the books were opened. What books? Well, the word Bible means books so it could be referring to the Bible. And John saw another book opened as well, which is the book of life. Then, all these dead people were judged by what was written in the first set of books mentioned, according to what they have done.

Now it's making more sense. God never punished Adam for his sins or Cain for killing his brother, and He didn't punish anyone for all the wickedness back in the day of Noah. And He never punished Satan. He was waiting until that Big Day of judgment. In the meantime, if you can't follow the rules, then GET OUT! That's not punishment, that's consequences. But then again, judgment is not punishment either. Judgment is where the light exposes those who are guilty.

Take another look at the timeline for a minute. Here we are on the Day of Judgment, the 1,000 years of peace have come and gone. The first resurrection happened 1,000 years earlier. And all those who died in Christ or those who believed in Jesus prior to the first resurrection were part of that first resurrection. All this happened a long time ago, long before the Day of Judgment and a long time before the books were opened.

The Bible talks about being saved and we've read several scriptures about that. But then we asked the question: "**saved from what?**". So, we searched the Bible to find out what it means to be saved. I only found two scriptures. One talks about being saved from the Wrath of God in **Romans 5:9 (ESV)** and the second one talks about NOT coming into judgment in **John 5:24 (ESV)** where it says, "Truly, truly, I say to you, whoever hears my word and believes him who sent me has eternal life. He does NOT come into judgment but has passed from death to life". Those who believe goes directly from death to life. They pass over judgment and avoid it altogether. In effect, they are "**saved**" from the Day of Judgment and the wrath of God.

Now here we are after the thousand years. Satan gets thrown into the lake of fire and the books were opened. Then John saw the second resurrection, the second harvest, the harvest of the ingathering. The sea gave up the dead, death, and hades (the grave) gave up the dead and now they were all judged according to what they have done. Then death and hades (the grave) were thrown into the lake of fire. Here we have Satan, the false prophet, the beast and now death and hades are in the lake of fire.

Remember earlier it was mentioned that death and hades were destroyed by Jesus' sacrifice. Death and hades getting thrown into the lake of fire could be symbolic of when Jesus destroyed them. Continuing in **Revelation** it says if anyone, whose name is NOT found in the book of life, would also be thrown into the lake of fire.

Wow! That is harsh. So, Adam, who's been dead for six thousand years, God's first human creation, the one who God said was **VERY GOOD**, gets resurrected for what? Just to be judged, yelled at, and then burned alive in the lake of fire. Adam has a special place in God's heart, he was His first human, how can God just watch his child, the one He loves, the one He formed with His own hands get burned alive like that. You try throwing your child into the fireplace or even your pet, your dog. That doesn't make any sense. Why not just leave him in the grave? He's already dead. Besides, Adam was just acting like a human, which is exactly how God made him.

But Wait!

1. Death and the grave were already destroyed, so these resurrected dead people can't die.

2. As we saw earlier, they don't have an immortal soul. So, they can't live either.

3. Besides, the lake of fire can't be Hell.
    - There was no mention of Hell in the Bible, except where the translators used an Old English word, but never in connection with a fiery pit where sinners go.
    - Not to mention, Jesus destroyed the works of the devil.

4. Also, we read earlier that Jesus paid the price for **ALL** sin. So, none of these people who do evil will be required to pay the price, since it's already paid.

- There are still consequences, but no penalty for sin, since the penalty was already paid.
 - Besides, we read that Jesus came to save the **entire** world.
 - And we read that when Jesus returns, He is only bringing salvation and not dealing with sin.

5. Also, we read about the Book of Life, which is opened after the 1000 years, but we don't really know what that is all about. The Bible never clarifies it. It just says **if anyone**, whose name is not found in the Book of Life would be thrown into the lake of fire.

So, what is it? This Book of Life. And whose names are in it and who's names are not found in the Book of Life? Although, you would think those found in the Book of Life would be the saints, the first fruits, those who believed. But they were already resurrected 1,000 years earlier. So, who are they? And why is the Book just now being opened? None of this is making sense!

Let's notice something interesting. We saw this earlier, but let's revisit it. Those, whose names were written in the book of life, were already there before God started with the creation of man. God already decided who would be in the book of life and who would not be in the book of life, long before Adam was even created. So, we don't really get a choice. It was already decided, pre-determined. All part of God's plan.

Let's look back at **Revelation 13:8 (ESV)**, "and all who dwell on earth **WILL** worship it (the beast), everyone whose name has not been written **before the foundation of the world** in the book of life of the Lamb who was slain".

That's right there in your Bible. I don't know if you can get any clearer than that. Those worshiping the beast were the same people whose names were NOT already written in the book of life. And when was that decided? **Before the foundation of the world**.

Just like Paul said in **Ephesians 1:3-4 (ESV)**, v3 "Blessed be the God and Father of our Lord Jesus Christ, who has blessed us in Christ with every spiritual blessing in the heavenly places, v4 even as He chose us in him **before the foundation of the world**, that we should be holy and blameless before Him. In love". God already chose us!

In other words, God already decided who would be holy and blameless and whose names would not be in the book of life before the foundation of the world. Everything was already mapped out, God came up with a winning game-plan, long before He created man. He didn't just leave it up to man to make things happen. God totally controls the game, who wins and who loses.

Then if we go back to **Revelation 17:8 (ESV)**, we also see whose names **HAVE NOT** been written before the foundation. It says, "The beast that you saw was, and is not, and is about to rise from the bottomless pit and go to destruction. And the dwellers on earth whose names have not been written in the book of life **from the foundation of the world** will marvel to see the beast, because it was and is not and is to come".

As you can see, once again, this is God's plan down to every detail. He does not leave anything to chance. He already knows who's written in the book of life and those who aren't. God is in control and we don't get much of a choice. The outcome has already been determined...God wins!

Then, the more I thought about the Book of Life the more I realized that God decided ahead of time who would be saved and who would be destined for the lake of fire. It was already decided whose names were written **before the foundation of the world.** Is God playing Russian Roulette with our lives? Then I'm thinking, that doesn't make any sense. That doesn't sound like God. Is He talking about literal names here? So, I decided to dig a little deeper.

Then, while taking a closer look, I found out when God says, **"whose names have not been written in the Book of Life"**, He is NOT talking about literal names. The word name or names is an English word, but the New Testament was written in Greek. So, the word "names" is translated from a Greek word which means your character or reputation. We still use similar expressions today. For instance, when we get out of High School or College, we might say, "I'm gonna move to the big city and make a 'name' for myself". We also refer to God as "Great is your name" or "Holy is your name". And, when Jesus returns, we read that the name by which he is called is "The Word of God". We can also see from the Old Testament that God gives us names based on our character, our reputation, just like He did with Jacob. His name meant deceiver or trickster. That was his reputation.

Basically, when God says, "whose names have not been written in the Book of life will be thrown into the lake of fire", He is referring to their character, their reputation. He is talking about the unrighteous, the ungodly, those who have not been born again…yet. Those known as team unbeliever. That is their name, the **NAME** of their team, their reputation.

Just like we read earlier where the Bible said the unrighteous will not inherit the Kingdom of God. So, who are they, those who have the reputation of being unrighteous? Well, we know, from the conversation with Nicodemus, that the only requirement for entering the Kingdom of God is that we be born again. So, everyone who was resurrected 1,000 years earlier must have already been born again. Therefore, those still lingering must be the unrighteous, not yet born again, those who are on team of unbelievers. They are called the "unrighteous", that is their **NAME**.

Then we see **Revelation 21:8 (ESV)**, where it says, "But as for the cowardly, the faithless, the detestable, as for murderers, the sexually immoral, sorcerers, idolaters, and all liars, their **portion** will be in the lake that burns with fire and sulfur, which is the second death.".

Who are doing these things? The unrighteous, the unbeliever. They have bad behavior; this is their reputation and what they are known for. They have not been born again or cleansed yet. So, their **portion** will be thrown into the lake of fire. What portion? Their unrighteous portion, which is not found in the book of life, will be cleansed in the lake of fire.

Think about the lake of fire for a minute. Some think it's Hell. Some think it is a fiery death trap. Most of the time when the word Hell was used it was in connection with Gehenna garbage dump. It was never used to describe the lake of fire. So, what is the purpose of the lake of fire? And why is it only mentioned four times in **Revelation**?

Well, first of all, the book of **Revelation** is full of symbolism, so this lake of fire must be symbolic along with the rest of **Revelation** and not meant to be a literal lake of fire. Although, some still think it is Hell. John never describes it as Hell. He sees what looks to him like a lake of fire. Besides, John has no idea what Hell is anyway. He never wrote about it in the Gospel of John or in I, II, III John. Not to mention, we really don't know what this lake of fire is, except we know it's symbolic. Does it go by any other names?

Yes, in **Revelation 20:14-15 (ESV)** it refers to the lake of fire as the second death. It says, "Then death and hades were thrown into the lake of fire. **This is the second death, the lake of fire"**. In other words, the lake of fire is also known as or called the second death. It **DOES NOT** say that people die a physical death and then get resurrected just to die a second time. That would be a waste of time and doesn't make any sense. Some people just assume that because they don't know what it means. Besides, we just read in **Hebrews 9:27 (ESV)** where it says, "it is appointed for **man to die once**, and after that comes judgment". It does not say after that comes **"a second death by fire"**, it says man dies **ONCE...** and after that comes judgment!

The second death is just another way to say the lake of fire, another name for it. Just like we say to God, "Holy is your name", we can say to the lake of fire, the second death is your name. Then, if anyone's name (group name, reputation, the unrighteous, the unbeliever) was not found written in the Book of Life, they would be thrown into the lake of fire." It **never says** they will die when they are thrown into this symbolic lake of fire. It just says, **the lake of fire is the second death**, in other words the lake of fire is called the second death.

All the images John is seeing are bizarre and symbolic of something. Some of which, the angel tells John what they mean and other images remain a mystery. However, in midst of all this symbolism and all these images it is unreasonable to think that all of sudden this lake of fire is suddenly a literal lake of fire or Hell. For one, it was only mentioned four times in **Revelation**, and we never heard about it until **Revelation 19**. So, why would it be literal when everything else about **Revelation** is symbolic? This may be one of those images that remains a mystery.

However, consider this...since death has been destroyed, Jesus already paid the price for all sin, and Jesus came to save the **entire** world, these newly resurrected people, who did not partake in the rewards of the first fruits / the first resurrection, have no place to go. Maybe God is not done with them yet. And He's going to throw these newly resurrected dead people into the lake of fire for cleansing and purifying. Not literally burning them up, but figuratively purging and cleansing their sin. This is all part of God's winning plan. It was also mentioned earlier that this same group of people who would be part of the second harvest, the second resurrection would be thrown into the great winepress of the wrath of God. So, which one is it? The winepress or the lake of fire? Actually both! They are both symbolic of the cleansing and purifying process.

Remember, Zechariah prophesied about this end-time fire. He kept referring to "On That Day", which indicates the end times or On That Day of Judgment. Then in **Zechariah 13:1 (ESV)**, the prophesy continues "On that day there shall be a fountain opened for the house of David and the inhabitants of Jerusalem, **to cleanse them from sin and uncleanness**". Now, this fountain will cleanse them from sin and uncleanness...On That Day.

And, since those who previously believed, those who are the first fruits are already saved, then who is God going to cleanse, On That Day? And since Jesus and the Holy Spirit is what cleanses us, then those who did not originally receive the Holy Spirit the first time around will need to get cleansed by the fire. Do they have to first believe? NO! The Bible never mentions that.

Then if we continue in **Zechariah 13:7-9 (ESV)** it prophesies more about the end time. It says v7 "Awake, O sword, against my shepherd, against the man who stands next to me, declares the Lord of hosts". Strike the shepherd, and the sheep will be scattered; I will turn my hand against the little ones. v8 In the whole land, declares the Lord, two thirds shall be cut off and perish, and one third shall be left alive".

It sounds like Zechariah is talking about the end time. Then in v9, he says "**And I will put this third into the fire**, and refine them as one refines silver, and test them as gold is tested. They will call upon my name, and I will answer them. I will say, **'They are my people'; and they will say, 'The Lord is my God'**".

Now we see that the surviving one-third will be tossed into the fire. Then, after God tosses them into the fire, they call upon His name and say, "The Lord is my God". **Wait a minute!** I thought God was going to destroy all the sinners in Hell or the lake of fire. Well, this might be true if God was going to lose in the end. But remember, God has a winning game plan.

Why are they thrown into the fire? Fire is symbolic and used as an analogy when Zechariah says God will put this one-third into the fire and refine them like silver and test them like Gold. It's not meant literally. Gold is full of impurities as it is mined and so are humans. So, God has to refine us. Those who have not yet been refined must go through the fire. Then, once they go through the fire, they will call upon His name...**ALL** of them. Once again, I do not see them getting a choice. God calls them His people and they **WILL** say "The Lord is my God". This is God's plan before man was created, before the foundation of the world. This is very much like the same analogy we saw earlier in **Malachi 3:2-3 (ESV)** in which fire was used to refine and purify.

Basically, in the Bible, you see fire used as a metaphor or an analogy to demonstrate the process that God uses to purify or burn off sin and cleanse us. God uses tests and trials in order to refine us just like the silversmith uses fire.

Notice that we only see the lake of fire mentioned three times until now and then one more time in **Revelation 21**. And the Beast, the False Prophet, Satan, death, hades, and now those not written in the book of life are thrown into the lake of fire.

Although, you don't hear about them getting burned alive, you don't hear about them dying, and you don't hear about them living eternal life in the fire. It just says they are thrown into the fire. Then after that, it's never mentioned again, so we still don't know what happened to all those resurrected people that were thrown in there except what God says in **Zechariah (ESV)**, "**They will call upon my name, and I will answer them. I will say, 'They are my people'; and they will say, 'The Lord is my God'**". God refers to them as His people, those who have been thrown into the fire.

And, along with everything else we've discovered about God's winning plan and the fact that fire is used in the Bible as an analogy for cleansing and purifying, it does make sense that God is using the fire to purge them from sin. So, what happens next?

Let's go to **Chapter 21** and see...

Revelation 21 (ESV) –
- John sees a new heaven and a new earth, and the old heaven and the old earth were passed away. Then he saw a new Jerusalem coming down from heaven, which he referred to as the Holy City. Then in v3, John heard a loud voice from the throne saying, "Behold, the dwelling place of God is with man. He will dwell with them, and they will be his people, and God himself will be with them"

Here we see that God is bringing His kingdom to earth. It's not exactly how we pictured it. Most people think that we will go to Heaven, but it doesn't look that way. God is bringing Heaven to us.

What about **John 14:2-3 (ESV)** where it says "In my Father's house are many rooms. If it were not so, would I have told you that I go to prepare a place for you? v3 And, if I go and prepare a place for you, I will come again and will take you to myself, that where I am you may be also".

Here we see Jesus going to prepare a place, which is true, but it doesn't say that place is in Heaven. He may be in Heaven working and preparing, but then He brings His kingdom to us. He said where He is there we will be also, which according to Revelation, he'll be returning earth.

Then we see God saying in v6-8, "It is done! I am the Alpha and the Omega, the beginning and the end. To the thirsty I will give from the spring of the water of life without payment. v7 The one who conquers will have this heritage, and I will be his God and he will be my son. v8 But, as for the cowardly, the faithless, the detestable, as for murderers, the sexually immoral, sorcerers, idolaters, and all liars, their **portion** will be in the lake that burns with fire and sulfur, which is the second death."

Look at all these evil things left in the lake of fire. Remember when John the Baptist was talking about the chaff getting removed and thrown into the fire. The Chaff was the unusable part of the wheat. The fire burns off the unusable parts of gold or silver in order to clear up the blemishes and purify the gold.

In v8 above it mentions all those who do these evil things and says their portion, the evil portion will be in the lake of fire. In other words that part of them. It doesn't say that anyone actually stays in the lake of fire, just their evil parts, the evil portion. Especially since Jesus already paid the price, so it's not like anyone is required or allowed to pay a penalty. They just have to get cleaned up a little. And remember it's the evil works that get burned up, but those who did those evil works will still be saved as explained in **I Corinthians 3:15 (ESV)** where it says, "If anyone's work is burned up, he will suffer loss, though **he himself will be saved, but only as through fire**"

In **Revelation 21:27 (ESV)**, it says "But nothing unclean will ever enter it, nor anyone who does what is detestable or false, but only those who are written in the Lamb's book of life". It's nothing unclean. Only those who have been cleansed whose names are in the Book of Life. Not specific names, but the **NAME** God gives to those who have been cleansed, whether He calls them "The Righteous", "The Believers", or something else.

According to **Revelation**, the names written in the Book of Life were written there before the foundation of the world. Keep in mind those that were part of the first resurrection, those that rose to meet Jesus in the clouds were already transformed 1,000 years before the book of life was even opened. If these were literal names, it would seem that those resurrected in the first resurrection would be the only names written, so why wait until after the 1,000 years to open it? That would not make sense. That's why we dug a little deeper to see what all this means.

Then, if you get to the end of the road and you are still unclean and full of unrighteousness, God is not going to let you in until you get a bath. That's where the symbolism of the lake of fire comes into play. By the many examples we've seen, fire is used as a way to cleanse and purify. Therefore, once you go through the fire you will be clean and ready to go.

God has a winning plan!

In the meantime, it looks like we are soon coming to an end of John's little adventure. Let's go to **Chapter 22** and see how things end up.

In **Chapter 22**, the angel was showing John the river of life flowing from the throne of God. On either side was the tree of life. Now this image is a little easier to figure out, especially since we see the river of life flowing from God. Then in v3 is the happy ending to the story where it says, "No longer will there be anything accursed, but the throne of God and of the Lamb will be in it, and his servants will worship him".

In the end, everything goes as planned, God wins. And now that John's home safe from his trip, the angel gives some final words of instruction.

The angel, who was sent with the message from Jesus, said Jesus was coming soon, the time is near, so don't seal up the words of the prophecy of this book. Let the evildoers be evil, let the righteous do right, and the holy be holy.

Then, just before concluding, the angel leaves him with this final warning. Don't add to these words and don't take away or there will be some seriously bad consequences.

SUMMARY

As you can see, there are a lot of things in the Bible that seem to get overlooked. They are right there in black and white, easy to understand, but a lot of people just breeze right by them.

One of the reasons these things get overlooked is because most of the time we start in the middle of the story...about the time when it's too late for man. By that time, man has already sinned, and we're all destined for Hell. Then we're thinking, had it not been for Jesus who swooped in at the last minute and saved the day, it would have been "curtains" for us! We would have been goners! We barely escaped the fiery pit by the "hair of our chinny chin chin"! Then we go through life with our head hung low, feeling guilty, low self-esteem, miserable. Thinking we disappointed God, we let Him down, thinking it's our fault Jesus was executed and that we caused Him to go through that terrible beating. Always feeling we are not worthy of God's love, kindness, and mercy, especially after we totally made a mess of things.

However, that is simply **NOT** true. Our story starts a long time ago. We had nothing to do with it. God had a plan long before He even created man. And that plan was to save everyone in the **WORLD**. He will stop at nothing to make that plan happen. God will do whatever it takes to finish the job. Hell will not stop Him, our bad choices will not stop Him, and rejecting God will not stop Him either. He will **NOT** let anything or anyone get in the way of finishing His plan and saving everyone in the **WORLD**, including those who reject Him.

God made man in their image, just like our children are in our image. God's plan is to re-create Himself through humans. God is creating a family! As for Adam messing up, that didn't change God's plan, that was God's plan. And our choice to reject God will not force God to change His plan either. After all, He designed us. God is actively working in the background to make sure His plan happens.

So, none of this is your fault! It's all part of God's plan. Jesus agreed to get executed long before man was even created. It was part of the plan. When we look at the big picture and go all the way back to the beginning, we can see that everything that God has done was intentional and by design. It's all part of His plan. You didn't ask to be here. So, lift your head up high, knowing God has a plan for you, which includes you messing up. You don't need to feel guilty or unworthy. God created each and every one of us for a purpose that fits into His plan. And there is nothing we can do to avoid it. Rejecting God will not stop God from fulfilling His plan in you. After all, it is God's plan! And He said that Jesus came to save the **WORLD**! That is His plan.

Then, as we took a journey back in the Garden of Eden to discover the mystery of man, we saw how amazing it was when some of those scriptures started to jump off the page. Then we continued all the way through to the symbolism of **Revelation**, where we saw more scriptures that have been previously overlooked.

By starting at the beginning of the story instead of in the middle, it gave us a solid foundation to continue exploring God's plan and His purpose for mankind. In the process, we discovered that a lot of what we've been taught about God and the Bible simply isn't true. So, we took a closer look to find out what the Bible actually says.

Let's take a minute to summarize a few things we learned in the process of separating the truth from the myth.

1. We saw that God is a planner and He came up with this great idea of creating a family. Which brings up several questions...
    a. **Did God plan on losing?** According to common belief, God will lose a lot of humans when they choose to reject Him. Was this part of God's losing plan?

b. **Maybe God is just a loser!** If God did not originally plan on losing, then what happened? Is God a loser?
c. **Is God smart enough to come up with a winning plan?** Since God is a planner and He designed the entire world and He designed man, He also anticipated that some humans would reject Him. Then He outsmarted them and came up with a way to save them anyway, in spite of themselves. God designed a winning game plan to guarantee salvation for **ALL** people. Besides, why go to all this time and trouble, pain, and suffering, including Jesus' sacrifice, just to lose in the end?

2. God gave man free choice! However, free choice is limited to the framework of God's plan.

    a. If God intentionally came up with a losing plan, then man's free choice would control God and dictate how His plan will turn out. He would be constantly changing and adjusting His plan every day.
    b. If God has a winning plan, then nothing we do, including rejecting God, will stop Him from saving everyone, the **ENTIRE WORLD**!

3. Then we saw that the Bible actually says in scripture that in Adam all die, but in Christ **ALL** shall be made alive. Whaaat! How can that be? This goes against everything we've been taught. But there it is, right there in your Bible.

4. Not only that, but we have also read scripture after scripture, that tend to get overlooked, such as God is patient and waiting until **ALL** come to repentance and **EVERY** knee will bow and **EVERY** tongue will confess Jesus. However, people often ignore it! Is God lying?

5. We also read scriptures that explained that everyone goes to the grave when they die, the abode of the dead, which means a waiting place. Waiting for what? Probably waiting for the resurrection. There is a resurrection to life and a resurrection to judgment.

6. In addition to that, we discovered that there is no such thing as an immortal soul. We searched the entire Bible and there is no mention of it, it's not even implied. The idea that we have an immortal soul that lives on after we die simply does not exist.

7. We also looked through the entire Old Testament and couldn't find any mention of Hell. Just a

Hebrew word that means Abode of the Dead. So, we decided to look into the New Testament for Hell.

8. In the New Testament, we did find Jesus talking about Hell. But when He mentioned it, He was **NOT** talking about a fiery pit where sinners go, He was referencing the Valley of Gehenna, a garbage dump just outside Jerusalem. It was the translators who used the Old English word Hell to describe the garbage dump. Then after Jesus died, Paul never wrote or preached about Hell...ever!

9. We also saw that fire is used symbolically as a way to purify and cleanse people of their sins. Not a tool for punishment.

10. Then, when we hear the word judgment or the day of judgment, we get these images in our head of fire coming down and consuming us as a way of punishment. But we learned that judgment or the day of judgment is **NOT** punishment or sentencing. It's just the method God uses to determine who is guilty and needs to be cleansed and purified with fire. Not punished with fire.

11. And we learned about the two harvests, the two resurrections. The first resurrection is for all those who believed in Jesus first, before everyone else.

God refers to them as the first fruits, they will rule with Christ a thousand years.

a. If we only have this one life to believe in Jesus and those that don't are lost forever, then why continue another thousand years after the resurrection. God is not done yet! There is another resurrection, there is another harvest, there are more people to purify and cleanse through the fire.

As you can see, God is very strategic, very intentional, He leaves nothing to chance. He is a planner. He has a well thought-out, well-organized plan. If we pick up the story in the middle where it is too late for man, the outcome seems horrific. Jesus tries to save everyone, but man's stubbornness is just too strong for Him, so He does the best He can, but in the end, He couldn't do it, He failed.

That is the way it appears on the surface. It looks like man controls God and His plan with our free choice. However, when we go to the beginning and see the big picture, we can see that God had a plan before man was even created. God's plan, God's will, God's choice. Our free choice does not dictate or control God's free choice. We only have free choice within the framework of God's plan. And if God says He's going to save the entire world, then "By God" He will save the entire world. Our free choice is NOT going to get in His way.

In fact, that is His plan...to save the entire world. His will is that all should reach repentance. He swore that every tongue shall swear allegiance. In Jesus all shall live. These are very clear statements. This is God's plan. There is nothing we can do to stop God from fulfilling His purpose and His plan to save the entire world. God has already put this plan into motion.

Even those who reject Jesus will not stop God from eventually saving them anyway. Whaaat? How can that be? Well, God has a plan and He **promised** He would save everyone...the whole world. Yet, you have that one dumbass, that one guy who is as stubborn as the day is long and He won't budge. This guy is holding up the line for the rest of us. Now God has Himself a dilemma on His hands. On one hand, God is not going to let this one guy into the Kingdom, unless he's been born again. Yet Jesus came to save the **whole world**. What does He do? At this point, God needs to figure it out. It's His plan. He needs to convince this guy to repent and turn towards Jesus. That is God's job, it is His responsibility to make this happen. He's the one who set all this in motion, came up with a plan and **promised** that in Jesus **ALL** shall be made alive!

I know this is not what you've been taught or what you've learned in church. It's not what I've been taught either. And I'm not just making this stuff up off the top of my head. It's NOT Randy's ideas or interpretation. Everything is right there in your Bible, in black and white.

Summary

Once you dig in and start reading or go back and re-read some of these scriptures with a new outlook, you will see that most of the Bible uses very clear statements, easy to understand. When you go back to the beginning instead of starting in the middle, you will begin to separate the truth from the myth.

Then you will be able walk around holding your head up high, knowing that God has your back and He has a purpose and a plan for your life. No matter what you've done, no matter what you do, God will always be there. There is nothing you can do to mess up God's plan for your life.

I hope and pray that God opens your eyes and blesses you with GREAT understanding. If you will pray and ask God as well, to open your mind, He is willing and ready to bless you. He may not flood you all at one time with new understanding, but you will start to have revelations, one "light bulb" moment at a time.

Thank you so much for taking the time to read this. I hope it blesses you and gives you a new and exciting outlook on God's overall plan for salvation.

© 2021 Randy Chesler
© 2022 Randy Chesler

CPSIA information can be obtained
at www.ICGtesting.com
Printed in the USA
BVHW070131121122
651754BV00008B/301